I AM SOMEBODY

A Memoir

Liam Ledwidge

New Generation Publishing

Cover design by Jacqueline Abromeit
Cover photograph by Furkan Yazici
Editing by Linda Harris

All profits from this publication go to charity.

"To experience the existence of spirituality and life itself, one must encounter pain as the touchstone to spiritual and human growth! Some people experience life to excess without all of its hardships, misery and depravity and I have been blessed to experience both! The wealth of experience is priceless and no money can ever charter its gain."

Liam Ledwidge

Dedications

To my late beautiful mother whose soul shone through her eyes
Josephine Lambe Ledwidge

&

My dear late friend
Yvonne Kelly Gibbons *(thank you for your encouragement)*
and her partner Ann O'Connor
whose friendship I treasure immensely

"Liam Ledwidge, Trailblazer"

Eamon Dillon, Ireland's 'Sunday World'.

"An Elder Statesman of his community"

The late Garry Ryan RTE 2FM

"Part of the core of I AM SOMEBODY is that it lingers. It hovers about in our mind long after we have read the text and then gently, and with reverence closed the book. It is indeed with reverence that we will close the cover of this book and tiptoe away in the knowledge that it is coming with us.

This book will get in on you. It is an account of one man's journey, a story that could so easily be laced with bitterness and self-pity, instead it oozes real hope and ultimate joy.

The greatest thing about this book is that it empowers. There are not too many things empower us to become the beautiful person we can be. Liam's story does just that. The phrase 'I AM SOMEBODY' will never be the same again. It's no longer a phrase but a battle cry for personal fulfilment."

Joe McDonald, Priest at Celbridge, Archdiocese of Dublin, Founder of Roncalli, a movement for the reform of the Church.

"An extraordinary story! It has been an honour and humbling experience to have worked with Liam…"

Linda Harris, Editor

ABOUT THE AUTHOR

Photo by: Furkan Yazici

Liam Ledwidge was once referred to as a *"Trailblazer"* by Eamon Dillon of Ireland's leading newspaper, *Sunday World.* He has lived a varied, interesting and challenging life working and travelling around the world and rubbing shoulders with colourful celebrities. Along with his former late partner, Tony Keogan, Liam was a high-profile personality in the Dublin business and entertainment sectors. Liam and Tony were partners for twenty-five years and were pioneers in the Irish commercial gay scene from 1975. They were the first gay couple to win the Dublin Chamber of Commerce Business Face Award 1993, for one of their enterprises – a guest house The Horse and Carriage.

Liam, joined by the world famous Danny La Rue and representing The Horse and Carriage, were the first gay entrants in Dublin's St. Patrick's Day parade on 17 March 1996. After a quarter of a century, Liam and Tony separated in 1999. Tributes of well wishes for the couple poured in after Liam's poignant interview on RTE's 2FM Gerry Ryan Show who said the couple had contributed so much to Irish society. Stephen Robinson of *Hot Press* wrote, "Earlier this year the gay community was shocked and saddened by the announcement by Liam Ledwidge that his 25-year relationship with business partner and lover Tony Keogan had ended." Such was the news, it seemed like a fairy-tale had ended. Tony died eight years later of natural causes.

In 2001, in a state of despair Liam moved to South Africa, where his sister and family lived, to set up a business. He was caught up in a web of lies, deceit, manipulation and accused of falsifying a marriage certificate to a Tamil widow which was absurd. He was robbed of in excess of one million rands (£100,00 in those days) and sentenced to three years' imprisonment in a notorious inhumane prison where he spent 77 days before the Court of Appeal released him, castigating the sentencing magistrate and the perpetrators of the crimes.

Liam's mother was in South Africa to witness the agonising crisis that befell her son. The trauma was challenging on her health and she became ill. He became her carer for the remainder of her life.

I AM SOMEBODY, is a compelling autobiography taking us through the journey of his life as a gay man to his many successes and the agonies of a prison hellhole. It is a compelling and powerful true story of lies, theft, torture, bloodshed, rape, suicide, death and corruption in South Africa where he was brutally incarcerated in Westville prison for a crime he did not commit.

Liam is also the author of the book *DANGEROUS PEOPLE DANCING INCOGNITO.*

I AM SOMEBODY

CHAPTERS

PROLOGUE

I was born on October 9th 1951, in the Old Coombe Hospital in an area affectionately known as 'The Liberties' in Dublin, Ireland, to William and Josephine Ledwidge. We first lived with my grandparents in Drimnagh, before moving to the inner city tenements in Chamber Street where I first attended school at nearby Weaver Square run by Catholic Nuns.

I lived there with my mother and father and baby sister Yvonne, in one room, whereas some families squeezed eleven or more into something similar. My father had divided the room with partitions and my mother had it immaculate but there was no getting away from the slums around us and the smell of the local abattoir was sickening!

In 1875, the greatest, most destructive fire that Dublin has ever seen crumbled most of the tenement buildings on Chamber Street, due to the Liberties Whiskey Fire. Pigs went squealing through the streets, horses bolted and became disorientated as the whiskey flowed like lava through the Liberties. When I went there to live with my parents in the early 1950s *(75 plus years later)* nothing had changed! The pigs were still squealing, the horses roamed the streets and the remaining Chamber Street Tenement flats were still standing.

In the middle of the 1950s my great-grandfather Farrell passed away and I was taken to see his remains at St. Kevin's hospital *(now St. James')* and to this very day I can still see him laid out in the mortuary in the dimly-lit almost draconian surroundings. I mention this in passing as one of the most mesmerising moments of my childhood projecting my own life, not knowing what lay ahead.

By 1956, we were now living in the west of the city in Ballyfermot, and by 1958, I started serving mass with the Dominican nuns in their private chapel which lasted for ten years. A remarkable spiritual experience which enhanced my Christian faith and has been tried and tested throughout the decades but more significantly in the bowels of hell in a prison in South Africa in 2002.

On a June morning in 1958, I remember a pungent smell emanating from the city brewery as it hovered like a foul mist over Dublin City, coupled with the beams of sunshine splitting the adjoining streets with their small clogged roof topped buildings leaving Bartley Dunne's *(public house)* on Lower Stephen's Street, in the silhouette of the sun. There was an odd spring in my step, which was ironic as my mother was taking me to Mercers Hospital *(next door to Bartley Dunne's)* with a flat foot! My foot was causing problems as my father had said that it would interrupt my football as I got older! I hated football! I knew little of my problem other than the fear I felt having to visit a hospital and meeting a man in a white coat called a 'doctor' and not knowing what to expect! I suppose I was hoping he was going to say, I must never be seen on a football pitch as it would damage my health! All of my uncles were into football and my grandfather had been a sergeant and physical training instructor with the Irish army! But me? I was a pussy cat in comparison! "Good Morning Mam," said a white-bearded gentleman to my mother as he patted me on the head whilst passing by and she greeted him accordingly! I was later to find out that it was Noel Purcell, a famous actor and movie star! I had seen a real live movie star and I was over the moon! "Does he know John Wayne?" I asked. *(John Wayne was the hero of many a movie goer as we used to watch him at the Gala Cinema, Ballyfermot in movies like Rio Grand and The Quiet Man.)*

"I'm sure he does sweetheart," replied my mother. I told all my friends that I had seen John Wayne but of course they didn't believe me! "Was he riding a horse?" asked one guy. "No," I said, "But I met Noel Purcell!" "Who's he?" came the reply and so the tale went on! There is a street in Dublin today called 'The Noel Purcell Walk' directly behind the College of Surgeons car park and within two minutes from where I met the great man himself. The club *INCOGNITO* I was to eventually open twenty-four years later with my late former partner, Tony Keogan, was set around the corner from the car park on Bow Lane East *(off Aungier Street)*. The club hit national and international news headlines when a Roman Catholic priest died there in 1994.

As the 1960s began, I was once again to experience death as my grandfather Ledwidge died aged 57 from cancer. He had been an upholsterer and a very good one at that! He was once commissioned to make a seat block for the presidential car for President Sean T. O'Kelly *(1945–1959)* and when it was finished he had to deliver it to Arus An Uachtarain *(House of the President)* in the Phoenix Park. When the great day arrived he took me with him and not only did the President shake my hand but he gave me a half crown as well!

On May 6th 1963, I was yet again to experience death when my great-grandmother Lambe, who had spawned

3

21 children, died at the age of 81, and in over two months later my beloved grandfather Lambe died aged 60! A pattern was beginning to emerge and it was to prove to me that life and death are part of living and we must embrace it with all of its consequences! It was the novitiate years of gaining inner strengths and resources in life which was to prepare me for the eventual tragedies that lay ahead.

Lights, camera, action was the name of the game when I entered showbiz in 1969, with the pseudo name Pat Peterson, under the directorship of the late Frank J Bailey, Artistic Managing Director of Amalgamated Artistes. It was here that I was to meet the *crème de la crème* of national and international stars of stage, screen and television which opened my eyes to freedom and liberty for the first time ever and in hindsight it was a golden nugget in education for my future life as a gay man and businessman!

In 1973, I was like a hamster in a cage and became totally infatuated with a footballer in London, who professed his undying love for me, and I fell head over heels for him only to be jilted which caused me to attempt the unimaginable 'suicide'. Having overcome this traumatic event I revealed my sexuality by coming out as gay in 1974, meeting the love of my life, Tony Keogan. In a relationship that spanned a quarter of a century, opening Ireland's first gay commercial night club 'Studio One' and then Mr Pussy's Nite Club in North Great Georges Street/Parnell Square in Dublin. It was during this period of time that we witnessed the rise in suicide amongst young gay men not being able to cope with their sexuality. One such man was our mechanic who after servicing our car drove his own car up to the

Dublin Mountains and committed the fatal act. We were shocked beyond words as he had left us in good humour. The shadow of suicide is frightening!

Tony and I went on to open the famous *INCOGNITO CLUB, The Horse & Carriage* Bed & Breakfast which won us the Dublin Chamber of Commerce Business Face Award in 1993, the first gay couple ever to win such an accolade. The death of a Roman Catholic Priest, in 1994, at *INCOGNITO* which catapulted us into world news headlines, the fire at *INCOGNITO* which some right wingers saw as punishment from the *hand of God* but proven wrong as the forensics said it was accidental.

We resurrected ourselves again and were the first gay entrant in the traditional 1996, St. Patrick's Day Parade in Dublin with the world's most famous female impersonator Danny La Rue. It was a treasurable, momentous and mad day partying with the former English footballer and Irish Football Manager Jack Charlton, at his pub 'The Baggot Inn' in Dublin. Then came the bleak and disastrous years as the split with my partner of twenty-five years caused me endless pain. I moved to South Africa where my sister, Yvonne, lived with her family, to set up a business but unbeknownst to us at the time powerful and influential South African friends of the family duped me into a marriage scam and robbed me of every penny from my working life in 2002. I was an innocent victim, guilty by persuasion and sentenced to a total of four years imprisonment of which I served 77 days until the court of appeal released me.

In a country embedded with conspiracy and corruption, I was mugged, beaten and robbed of my entire wealth. I was now mingling not only with thieves and vagabonds but murderers, rapists including baby rapists, schizophrenics, drug crime lords and their victims, HIV/AIDS sufferers and one poor man who stole a chicken in order to feed his family. I was constantly in fear of my life in the midst of evil prison gangs (made up of 26- and 28-year-old men) formed over 100 years ago with total allegiance to their hero and founder Nongoloza Mathebula. It was the most obnoxious, depraved pit in the bowels of hell that I had ever experienced. A place of desolation, ruination and desecration of mind, body and soul. My dearest mother who witnessed the conspiracy and corruption visited me in prison along with our lifelong friend and neighbour, Maureen, who were to say the least heartbroken and devastated. It was extremely distressing for my sister Yvonne, and my South African family and friends. My mental state was at an all-time low and my physical well-being was deteriorating on a daily basis. I was an utter wreck!

The extreme pressure on my mother was devastating throughout the travesty but it is unimaginable to encapsulate her deep disappointment at a scurrilous report by a common hack in an Irish Evening Newspaper implicating the former President of Ireland, Mary Robinson, with me. The inaccurate details made sensational reading which sickened her to the pits of her stomach. In the shadow of the controversy, my mother became a shadow of her former self and when I landed back in Ireland, I will never forget the saintly serenity on her face; the sadness we felt that those we had helped, those so-called friends and show business friends were nowhere to be seen and as her illness progressed I was her carer/minder for the rest of her life until her passing in May 2016.

During the twelve years of caring for my beloved mother, my time was limited but I wrote my book *Dangerous People Dancing Incognito* occasionally granting an interview to people like Lloyd Newson, *DV8* from Australia, *The South African Sunday Times,* Eamon Dillon of *The Irish Sunday World, Gay Community News,* and other local media including Edmund Lynch's television documentary *A Different Country.'*

In 2007, my former partner of 25 years, Tony Keogan, died suddenly and this tragedy plunged me into deeper despair only to be rescued by my deep faith coupled with the intense love I had caring for my mother. It was a resurrection of my spiritual baptism which I had experienced with the Dominican Nuns as an altar boy all those years ago. To experience the existence of spirituality and life itself, one must encounter pain as the touchstone to spiritual and human growth! Some people experience life to excess without all of its hardships, misery and depravity and I have been blessed to experience both! The wealth of experience is priceless and no money can ever charter its gain.

I am now ready to tell my unique story in a journey that will take you from the beginning until I gained personal peace in my own lifetime by being able to forgive those who harmed me.

ONE

Baptism of Fire

The scourge of the belt, cane and sometimes fist were the nightmare of many pupils who attended the De La Salle Brothers in Ireland of the 1960s. I was the victim of such an attack in 1961, when I was punched, belted with a strap and kicked in the groin by a religious madman as my nervous system was shattered when he screamed and roared at me like a gorilla, with his tongue clenched between his teeth and his insane wide eyes penetrating through me. It was terrifying! I was admitted into Cherry Orchard Hospital suffering under the guise of 'glandular fever'!

My grandfather, an ex-army sergeant, was having none of it and went in search of this religious brother but he refused to see him! Instead he apologised to my mother saying that he had 'gotten' out of the wrong side of the bed that morning! My father was furious and wanted to take the matter to a higher authority and an eventual court hearing through a relative who worked at the Department of Education! However he was advised not to proceed as it was unheard of to prosecute a religious in a court of law! After all, this was the land of Saints and Scholars! This brother was a mad, psychotic, dangerous and frustrated individual who physically and mentally abused me and went on to commit similar attacks on other young boys! He should never have been allowed into religious life and certainly not into the teaching profession! He was eventually sent to the missions in Africa where he died. My family never took the matter any further due to the dominant role of the Catholic Church in Ireland at that time and I never pursued the matter in later years.

Catholicism was booming in the country in the 1960s and every seminary, monastery and convent was filled to capacity. Men and women bowed down to their clergy and were often in fear of the controlling grip they had on the nation! As an altar boy with the Dominican nuns, I experienced nothing but goodness and my ten-year tenure with them was spiritually rewarding.

I guess by 1963, maturity of sorts was beginning to emerge within me and I felt the urge of male company, but I was living in a conservative dominated Catholic country where priests lectured us from the pulpits with insane screaming voices denouncing sexual acts and sex before marriage as a mortal sin and we would all be damned to hell! In the 1960s I was trying to face up to maturity by realising that I was gay, but what chance did I or my peers have with a satanic element within the church who openly saw homosexuality as EVIL and an offence towards the Almighty when they themselves were acting out deviant acts of sexual deranged depravity on young men!

This frightened and scared many people leaving them mentally wrecked, confused and insecure, resulting in many psychological problems. They also lectured that sex outside of marriage was the ultra-betrayal of God, and Satin was waiting in the wings for these evil mothers and their bastards! What a statement to make! It made life depressing and embarrassing resulting in depression, addiction to alcoholism, drug abuse and suicide which was also a mortal sin in those days!

Families lived precarious lives, afraid of priests and nuns while some priests and bishops would arrange for the "fallen woman" to enter a home protected by the nuns and when the child was born it was put up for adoption mainly by wealthy Americans as depicted in the movie *Philomena* starring Judy Dench. The women languished tirelessly in laundries run by the nuns later to become famously known as *The Magdalene Laundries*.

It was alleged that young male criminal offenders were sodomised by Christian brothers and priests, and a report published in 2009 stated that back in the 1940s, many children in Industrial schools in the Republic, had been subjected to systematic and sustained physical, sexual and emotional abuse. It also found that the perpetrators of this violence had been protected by their religious superiors, primarily out of self-interest to maintain the reputation of the institutions concerned. The male-dominated Roman Catholic Church was and is a misogynistic world organisation where even nuns are considered inferior to priests, which is extraordinary when the Mother of God is revered the world over as is St. Therese of Lisieux along with countless other women.

The abuse that these anointed religious inflicted on these young men and women was not only criminal and hypocritical but perverse to the extreme and an indelible mark on the side of the Irish Catholic Church, least of all on the Irish nation as a whole.

These atrocities, unbeknownst to me and the general public at the time, have over the decades been dissected and bitterly digested by the whole world, but for me and my own personal experiences it was a baptism of fire and a long trial of personal faith and resurrected in the bowels of hell in a prison in South Africa in 2002.

The confessional is supposed to be a source of spiritual and mental comfort where penitents confess their sins to an ordained priest of God. However, in Ballyfermot of the 1960s it was terrifying! Overworked, quirky elderly clergy were aggressive and frightening in their tone and attitude which was terrifying and sent a chill down the spine.

"Daly get your hands out of your pockets!" roared the priest from an open-curtain confessional as he kept an eye on the waiting pupils, whilst he simultaneously heard confessions from terrified young men at the Church of the Assumption in Ballyfermot in 1964. "You what?" we heard him roar, "Mother of God! Five decades of the Rosary," and he mumbled the blessing whilst slamming the sliding grid door. All eyes turned on the terrified red-faced pupil as he exited the confessional on his way up the church to start his repentance and to say his five decades of the rosary. It was like a circus, as you didn't know what was coming next! I knew all of the priests including the famous Parish Priest, Canon Troy *(who it was believed married one of the 1916 leaders, Joseph Mary Plunkett to Grace Gifford in Kilmainham Jail hours before his execution by the British)* who celebrated mass from time to time at the Dominican Convent. Canon Troy was a great visionary and believed ostensibly in family life. He was a staunch republican and an awkward cranky man who wouldn't entertain the youth of the parish playing soccer! I never agreed with him and I would challenge him resulting in him referring to me as 'the cheeky lad'. However, I had great respect for him and I showed this respect when dealing with him. He liked that and as a result, I had a great affinity with him; when he visited the convent to say mass, he would request three crucibles of red wine instead of the traditional one and this was 7.30 in the morning! He knew that I was different and one day he said to me, "Liam, I will absolve you of your sin but you must confess to Fr. Ryan *(name changed)* and he will bless you and you will enter the Kingdom of Heaven at the end of your life!" I thanked the good Canon and a few days later, I went to Fr. Ryan who looked like a comedy actor *(*Dick Emery*)* with prominent teeth. I proceeded, "Bless me Father for I have sinned, it's been a week since my last confession," I said. "Yes my son," he retorted. "Father I think I'm Queer and I need absolution!" There was silence and then there was a burst of pontifical eloquence "In Nomine Patris et Filii Spiritus Sancti." He blessed me and said, "Repeat" and so I repeated myself to which he replied, "We all feel out of sorts from time to time but I suggest you get your mother to give you two pain killers and you will be as right as rain in no time!" He blessed me once again and that was the end of the matter!

Those early priests in Ballyfermot were hard-working men who didn't think twice about clipping an ear or two of the local bullies or smart individuals who thought they were hard men. They were honest and overworked but none of them held liberal views, at least not in public, but there were one or two who were very fond of the drink! By the time I left Ballyfermot in the early 1970s there had been no scandals, but coming down the track was the notorious Tony Walsh who sexually abused boys as young as 8 years of age in the rooms and grounds which we considered sacred. My stomach churned at the national scandal, and the elderly clergy including nuns, priests and brothers who had done no wrong and had dedicated their lives to God and their profession were humiliated. This was a monster let loose under the guise of a 'Singing Priest' who was a cohort of another religious falter, Fr. Michael Cleary whom I'm ashamed to say I detested at the time.

In the early 1980s, my late former partner Tony Keogan and I had been informed through senior church authorities who were members of our club *INCOGNITO* that Michael Cleary had fathered a child or two! Cleary heard that I was aware of the allegations and tried to discredit me. It was the greatest mistake of his life! Our solicitors convened and a strong strenuous letter was sent to Cleary at his residence. Cleary denied the allegations he made against me and promised to fight the matter tooth and nail! We sent a second letter to inform him that proceedings were being prepared by council against him and we would see him in court.

Thirty-six hours later I received a telephone call from a long-standing friend of mine who was a Dominican nun in Ballyfermot. She asked if I could meet her as a matter of urgency as it involved Fr. Michael Cleary. I hesitated for a while, but because I had known her for many years I agreed to meet her on condition that Tony accompanied me. She agreed.

I drove from the city centre with Tony to my old stomping ground, the Dominican Convent in Ballyfermot. I can still hear the gravel stones beneath the car as we pulled up outside the convent. As we approached the entrance, the door swung open and we were led into a side parlour of which I was familiar with and where we were offered tea or coffee with biscuits. My dear friend entered in a stressful state, with her red cheeks contrasting against her white habit. She had met Tony several times before and the last time we had met was in 1979 when we brought her a present from Rome blessed by Pope John Paul II prior to his visit to Ireland in September of that year. I knew by her demeanour that she was nervous and I had never seen her like that before. She thanked us for agreeing to meet her and I interrupted her by telling her to get to the point about Cleary.

She looked at me with those angelic eyes and said, "Liam, I know you are very upset and I understand that these allegations are damaging. I have no problem with Tony and neither has any of the sisters with whom you served with total dedication for ten years. However, we are in dangerous territory as Fr. Cleary is very upset and remorseful. I am pleading with you to forgive any transgression!"

I knew instantly that she was under pressure and the last thing I wanted at that time was to see her upset. I asked her what she wanted me to do and her eyes lit up and she replied, "Just listen to what he has to say." I agreed and told her to relay our message to Cleary and our solicitors would reply accordingly. She became over anxious and said, "But he's here," to which Tony replied "O' let's get on with it!"

Within a blink of an eye, Michael Cleary was ushered in looking like a shadow of his former self. This was a man who was known nationally as a singing priest, who courted show business personalities, who loved his drink and cigarettes, sports cars and who a few years earlier had stood on the podium with the disgraced Bishop of Galway welcoming Pope John Paul II, and here he was practically on his knees in front of me seeking forgiveness. I was acutely aware that he knew of our knowledge in relation to his affair with Phyllis Hamilton but I watched him that night grovelling before us and saying, "For any indiscretion on my part I am sincerely sorry, I am asking forgiveness," at which point Tony said, "Get out of my sight!"

He tried to interrupt but I reiterated what Tony had said adding, "Go your pathetic way and may God forgive you. For your own peace of mind the matter is now closed." He couldn't get out of the room quick enough. My dear friend the Dominican nun kissed me with delight saying, "Don't worry boys! God will deal with him!" I was never to see my Dominican friend again as she died six months later at the age of 48!

Cleary was to survive another ten years and, in my opinion, he was the most despicable member of the clergy that ever walked! I have always regretted the fact that we never pursued him for justice and it was always a bone of contention between Tony and I who would have gone for him at the drop of a hat! It was jaw-dropping to see personalities employed by the National Broadcaster bowing down to a man ordained as a priest, who lived the life of a pop star and drove sports cars, fathered children, drank like a fish, was a consummate smoker and a hypocrite that went against all of the rules of the organisation he was a member of, the Roman Catholic Church. Here he was, a man who tried to discredit gay life whilst mixing with gay people on the showbiz circle; he tried but failed and fell at the last hurdle! Tony and I received a telephone call upon receipt of his death and there was no love lost.

However, all of this including the scandals reminded me of St. Therese of Lisieux, *(1873–1897)* in a worldwide best-selling autobiography *The Story of a Soul*. Referring to Roman Catholic Priests, she wrote, *"We are to pray for them while they are preaching to souls through their words and especially their example. I must stop here, for were I to continue I would never come to an end!"*

The people of Ireland especially the older generation were to suffer greatly as the years progressed as one church scandal followed another. Their faith was shaken to the core. It was a tsunami that would eventually see the end of the dominance of the Roman Catholic Church's stronghold on the Irish nation. However many years were to follow and like a forgotten World War II bomb, the scandals would explode!

However, back in the mid 1960s a change of culture was taking place with the emergence of The Beatles, and the Summer of Love in San Francisco. In 1967, a collection of hippies who were opposed to general rule and opposition to the Vietnam War made loud noises around the world and a breath of fresh air was realised. I remember I was extremely excited at this new reformation as I saw it as a new gateway to liberalisation. For the first time we began to see the publications of gay literature although we in Ireland had to sit back for a short while until some brave men and women united in forming the Irish Gay Rights Movement and the emergence of David Norris.

In the mid to late 1960s, colloquial terminologies were more frequently used when referring to gay people as 'Queers' 'Faggots' 'Steamers' 'Shirt Lifters' to name but a few, and although not quite uncommon today even after Ireland introduced marriage equality in 2015, homophobia is very much alive and imbedded in the minds of some! However, back then it was a life of crucifixion which entailed many young men committing suicide; others were sent to see psychological therapists with severe anxiety and depression or even the local priest for direction! It resulted in an assembly of confused and perplexed personalities many of whom gave up and got married, had children and cruised city cottages *(public toilets)* for gay sex! Married men would pay 'Rent Boys' for sex picked up on quaysides, parks, sand dunes on local beaches, or wherever they could get it. The Gardaí would frequently raid these places and sometimes prosecutions entailed, and on other occasions interferences from unknown authorities would prevail and the charges would be dropped. One way or the other it brought massive shame and humiliation on the individual but this was protocol and a sign of the times back in those dark bleak and dreary days.

There are many men in Ireland today who are married with grown-up children who are bisexual, who have proven themselves to be good fathers but cheating husbands! They live a life of *INCOGNITO but* no-one has the right to be judgemental as we all have skeletons in our closet!

However, for all of their faults the majority of the clergy in the Roman Catholic Church were good, honest, decent individuals who served the Irish nation well and gave a second-to-none superb education to our citizens for which we should be truly grateful. I often reflect with sadness about the idealism of these great men and women who were never given the opportunity to marry which would have made their lives far healthier, secured and would have reflected in the administration of their duties. If the stagnant attitude of Rome continues, the already fallen church will sink like the *Titanic* but the spirit of Christ will always live on and I firmly believe that the Church of Rome is approaching the eve of a great reformation in decades to come!

Two

Staircase to an Open World! Showbiz and Irish Theatre!

By 1968, I had been involved in youth affairs and I had a great relationship with the Dominican Order between St. Mary's in Tallaght, Dominick Street and of course my ten-year tenure as an altar boy with the Dominican nuns in Ballyfermot. As my time was coming to an end with the nuns, a visiting Dominican priest Fr. T.P. McInerney who came to celebrate mass was received in total amazement especially by the altar boys as he was covered in makeup! One boy said, "Jasus, he looks like me granny!" The nuns tippy toed around him whilst others made jokes but, to my amazement, I was summoned to his breakfast parlour and asked to go on his Irish television show 'People Are Asking'. A teenage topical programme discussing the issues of the day but instead of asking the questions I wanted to ask, I was handed a list of questions to present!

The show, which was recorded in Studio Two at Montrose, was successful and so I was asked back a second time with two other boys. The answers got mixed up, with one boy complaining that he was unfairly treated and the recording should be scrapped! The complaint was dismissed out of hand and the recording went ahead. I was invited back for a third time without anyone else from my group and it was here that I began an affinity with the floor manager Alan Gibson who was gay. He invited a friend and me to an apartment in the leafy Dublin suburb of Rathgar, where he modelled modern underwear for a half an hour. We were mesmerised and laughed continuously, probably because of nerves and the unknown! He invited me back out to the RTE Studios *(Irish television and radio)* to watch him in action as floor manager for the 'Late Late Show' plus many other programmes including the recordings of 'Steady as She Go Goes' with Maxi, Dick and Twink directed by Bill Keating.

I was always in awe of Gay Byrne who presented the world's longest running chat show, 'The Late Late Show'. He was a consummate professional and way ahead of his time, having brought up controversial matters on his show such as Gay Rights, Abortion, the Church's role in modern society and Lesbian Nuns to name but a few! He did more for Ireland by opening people's minds than any church or government body ever did and he didn't suffer fools easily! Ireland suffered a great loss when Gay Byrne died on 04 November 2019. May he rest in peace.

By 1969, Alan approached me again and asked me to join his newly formed company Amalgamated Artistes, situated at 18 Kildare Street across the road from the Irish seat of Parliament, The Dáil. I accepted!

I was introduced to the Artistic Director Frank J. Bailey, an arts graduate from Galway University, a theatre actor/director and producer from Radio Eireann, *(Irish Radio)*. He was an affable kind-hearted man with a serious visionary approach to Irish theatre. He was often flamboyant and very theatrical, referring to people as 'Dear Heart' but I was soon to get used to this as it was common practice amongst the show business fraternity.

I was employed as his Personal Assistant and every evening he would take me to the Shelbourne Grill at the world famous Shelbourne Hotel overlooking Stephen's Green or the Trocadero Restaurant for dinner where I got to meet the *crème de la crème* of show people. It was a world of excitement and my first insight into gay life as gays mingled with stars openly without any comments, it was like we were living in a different world!

Amalgamated Artistes had leased the Eblana Theatre in Busarus *(a theatre in the underground of a Dublin bus station)* in Dublin City centre, and their first production was the play *Joe Egg* starring Lynn Furlong of 'Z Cars' and 'The Avengers' television shows. The opening night was spectacular with the cream of Irish Theatre in attendance including the famous actors/directors Michael MacLiammoir and Hilton Edwards. I was introduced to the couple by Frank Bailey and I remember Michael saying to Hilton, "Hasn't he got beautiful eyes?"

I was also introduced to the fabulous Irish actress Siobhan McKenna and many years later she was to re-introduce me to Danny La Rue in the Mermaid Theatre in London when she was starring in *Playboy of the Western World*.

As Personal Assistant to Frank, I was also the receptionist at Amalgamated Artistes and I would be required to work late into the night. One evening I was alone in the offices when there was a knock on the door and when I answered it there was a man standing there with his back to me on the darkened stairwell who immediately turned around, almost sinister-like, and frighteningly said, "Good evening!" I stared at him for a moment and replied, "Good evening, can I help you?"

"I'm looking for Mr Bailey, I was just passing by and thought that we might have a chat for a moment." I told him that Frank would be back momentarily if he cared to take a seat. He entered and in the lightened office I recognised him immediately as the Hollywood Actor O.Z. Whitehead, famous for his role in John Ford's movie *The Grapes of Wrath* alongside Henry Fonda and who had appeared in movies with John Wayne, Hayley Mills including many more, and on stage with Katherine Hepburn.

"I'm sorry Mr Whitehead, I didn't recognise you in the dark! Can I get you tea or coffee?" He spoke very softly and replied, "No thank you dear boy, it was courteous of you to mention that you recognised me, some people are scared of me!" He wasn't joking as I was trembling, but as time went by I got to know him better and he was a real gentleman.

On another occasion I was to meet a young singer/songwriter Chris Davison, later to become world famous as Chris De Burgh. He would come in and out of the offices to see Frank, to discuss a musical he had written which never materialised, but he was always very courteous towards me.

Frank lived on Northumberland Road, in Dublin 4, and on many occasions I would be invited to his apartment. One evening he said to me, "I want to make you into a top disc jockey and host a spectacular pop show called 'Pop in the Sun' at the National Stadium!" I was dumbfounded! I thought I was dreaming. "Are you for real?"

"Dear heart," he replied, "Your time has come! We will give you the stage name of 'Pat Peterson' and I have arranged for voice projection lessons with Betty Anne

Norton, in Harcourt Street." I was absolutely overwhelmed with excitement and he said, "I have set up a meeting tomorrow for you to meet some rocker who called me the other day seeking an agent! Dear heart, just listen to his advice, he's a few years older than you but I think he may have potential!"

"Who is this rocker?" I asked.

"Phil Lynott is his name, we will meet him at our offices tomorrow; put him in for 5pm," he said.

I had heard about this up-and-coming artiste from gigging around town, but I wondered how he was going to help us. The following day arrived and in walked Phil Lynott with guitar in hand. He was a very down-to-earth guy with no bullshit and we chatted briefly with him wishing me luck for the big night.

Frank arrived five minutes late *(he liked to keep people waiting)* and in his usual manner he greeted Phil by saying, "Dear heart, sorry to have kept you waiting! Please come into my office." Phil strolled into Frank's office at which time the telephone rang and I excused myself to answer the call and within minutes I joined them in the main office. Frank said, "Dear heart, this young man is seeking an agent and I'm interested but I'm also hungry, let's go across the road."

We all went across the road to the Shelbourne Grill. Frank told me that Phil had said that the line-up for 'Pop in the Sun' was lacking 'dynamism' which Frank didn't like and so he invited him back to the office where he said, "Sing me a song with your guitar," and Phil obliged accordingly with a rock version of a popular song. I knew instinctively that Frank was horrified as he saw this as a great insult to the famous song. There was a knock on the door and it was an uncle of mine to pick me up. I shook hands with Phil Lynott and apologised to Frank who was disgusted that I was leaving. "Never mind, dear heart, I'll have an early night on my own!" He was annoyed!

The following day Frank arrived at the office, very cheerful, wearing a pink blazer, and so I asked how the meeting ended up and he replied sharply, "Not my cup of tea darling! Not my cup of tea!" I was never to see Phil Lynott again but, to my greatest delight, Phil became a world famous rocker as lead singer with Thin Lizzy with some great hits like 'Whiskey in the Jar' and 'The Boys are Back in Town'; he died so young on the 4th January 1986. Today there is a statue of him on Dublin's Harry Street where, only a stone's throw away from Kildare Street, Frank Bailey had dismissed him. It's not any Tom, Dick or Harry who gets this privilege!

On a beautiful summer's evening we took a break and strolled through Stephen's Green, when out of the blue Frank said that he had a surprise for me but we needed to get back to the office. When we got back he said he needed to be alone in his office but to listen for a knock on the door. Twenty minutes passed and there was a knock on the door, which I answered and was greeted by: "Hello Liam!" It was the great Irish/Hollywood actor Peter O'Toole, whom Frank Bailey had given my name to in order to surprise me! Frank then emerged laughing like a hyena! The three of us went to the Trocadero Restaurant where head waiter Frank was tripping himself up in awe of Peter O'Toole.

There was more excitement to follow as Frank informed me that we were both going to London with Alan Gibson to see some West End Shows and he wanted me to gain experience by seeing the professionals in action. It was beginning to dawn on me that this was serious and I needed to focus at all times. I never drank or smoked in those days, which was a help. Frank said to me that he wanted to make me a star on one condition that I never entered Bartley Dunne's pub as it was full of men who would only want to seduce me! I had never been inside the establishment at that time so it didn't bother me.

The day arrived and we travelled to London checking into the Lancaster Hotel; it was my second trip to the British capital but I had never been to the West End. That night we went to see the *Man of La Mancha* musical and afterwards to a showbiz restaurant where Sir John Gielgud was sitting opposite and across the way was Hollywood's famous actress Lauren Bacall. I was blown away!

The next day we did a tour of the great London sights and that night we went to the London Palladium to see Des O'Connor, and Frank told me to watch his moves and how he handled the microphone as it was imperative for my future career! I had already mastered the microphone and as for singing, I couldn't sing to save my life! However my dad was a great singer and in the 1950s toured the country with his singing partner Austin Gaffney. Austin went on to become professional but my dad decided otherwise and got a 9-to-5 job.

After the Des O'Connor show, Frank informed me that we were going to the Danny La Rue Club in Hanover Square. Danny La Rue was a famous female impersonator who attracted all of the stars including its most famous patron the Queen of England's sister, Princess Margaret. However, when we got there the club was closed for some reason and so Frank as usual insisted that we go to this other club where Danny La Rue was holding court with friends and admirers. Frank eventually brought him down to our table where I was introduced to him with Alan Gibson. Danny exclaimed "My God we're all from Ireland, he's from Galway, I'm from Cork and don't tell me you two are *Dublin Jackeens!* Ha! Ha!" in that famous laugh of his! I immediately jumped in and said, "Mr La Rue" at which point I was interrupted, "Dan, please, we are all friends here."

"Dan," I said, "Why don't you come to Ireland for a show?" "Simple, my dear, I'm extremely busy and secondly they couldn't afford me! Anyway you have the great Maureen Potter and Siobhan McKenna." The conversation ended and he went back to holding court! I was unaware at that time that many years later we were to become friends and become the first two gay people to enter the St. Patrick's Day parade in Dublin sponsored by British Midland Airways in 1996.

Ronnie Corbett who was a young star frequently appeared at Danny La Rue's club in Hanover Square and was a lifelong friend to Dan along with his wife Anne. Ronnie went on to become famous as one half of The Two Ronnie's with Ronnie Barker. He was a delightful man to meet.

The following night we went to see the controversial musical 'HAIR' after its launch in New York which had a scene of full nudity, a brave step even for London in 1969.

The next day I was taken to Carnaby Street for my new wardrobe as Pat Peterson. Frank had 'Pop in the Sun' in mind and so a white suit, shirts, trousers, a red cape and a wig was bought! He insisted that my hair was too short and I needed a style like the Beatles!

The shopping was finished and the magical visit to London was over and so we flew back to Dublin. Whilst 'Joe Egg' was still running at the Eblana we went straight into rehearsal for 'Staircase' starring the wonderful David Kelly and Godfrey Quigley. Both men were great actors but I always remember David Kelly being very kind to me. David went on to huge international success starring in many popular British and Irish television productions such as 'Fawlty Towers', 'Robin's Nest', 'Emmerdale' and 'Strumpet City' to name but a few.

In my new role as Pat Peterson I was making guest appearances around town, gigging here and there; it was tough going along with all of my other duties but I enjoyed it. I got a gig with *Spotlight Magazine* to judge the final of their disc-jockey competition at Butlin's Holiday camp in Mosney, County Meath with a top prize of a Honda 50 motorcycle.

When the day arrived I was in agony with a wisdom tooth and I couldn't rid myself of the pain but I carried on as best I could. I was told that a make-up artiste would arrive at the offices at 5pm and another new outfit had been bought for me to wear on the night. Frank was very kind to me giving me pain killers and kept saying, "It's too late for him to go to a dentist as he will not be able to do this important gig tonight!" I reassured him that I would be alright and I wasn't prepared to let the team down. "That's my boy! That's my trooper!" he said.

The makeup artiste arrived who was a very camp man and applied the make-up telling me that it had a staying power of eight hours! I donned my new outfit, as Alan Gibson informed me that the Rover was outside and he would take me to Butlin's. Frank wasn't travelling with us but he wished me well and so I went downstairs to get into the Rover. "Sit in the back!" Alan Gibson said sternly, "and act like a star!"

We drove to the Malahide Castle en-route to pick up Alan's partner Clem who came rushing out with cotton wool and miniature bottles of whiskey. "Now dear, listen to what the nurse is saying, I am going to apply the whiskey to the cotton wool and you must insert it over the tooth and bona! My love." I did as required several times and the taste of the whiskey was sickening! However, we arrived at the Holiday Camp with Alan Gibson, informing the Entertainments Manager that there should be no delays, as we had a midnight appointment in Dublin. I privately told the manager to take his time. I was then introduced to the finalists before going on-stage. They were a lovely enthusiastic bunch of guys who looked at me in awe dressed to the 'nines' who had read about me every week in *Spotlight Magazine*. One guy kept staring me which made me nervous but the time had arrived and I was introduced with much fanfare to the visitors and holiday residents. I went on and spoke a few words, then went into the audience to see who their favourite winning DJ was and then I introduced the finalists. They all appeared on stage to much applause and went on to spinning their discs. I was given a forty-five minute break to make up my mind. In all fairness to Clem, he kept applying the whiskey onto the cotton wool for my aching tooth whilst Alan kept saying, "I think you should choose this one or that one," with Clem telling him to, "shut the fuck up, Pat will decide!"

It's important to understand that I never knew any of these disc jockeys and my first meeting with them was on that night. I went back on stage naming the two runners-up and then the finalist is "Tony Keogan!" This was the guy who had been staring at me earlier which had no bearing on my decision. The Honda 50 was wheeled on and presented. He informed us that he was from Rialto, in Dublin, and I wasn't to see him again until five years later when we fell in love and lasted a quarter of a century. This was a man who unintentionally was shadowing me as a child growing up, and we were both unaware that fate had been dawning!

In the meantime back at HQ in Kildare Street and with three weeks to go before 'Pop in the Sun', news filtered through from ticket agents that sales were poor! Frank and his co-directors became very nervous and ordered several full-page advertisements in *Spotlight Magazine* and I was rushed down to the GPO where Radio Eireann *(Irish Radio)* was then situated before moving to Montrose in Donnybrook to do interviews with Terry Prone on the 'Young Idea' radio programme. Frank went to do an interview with Terry Wogan, and the great Terry really plugged it! We were delighted with all the interviews we did.

After the interview with Terry Wogan, Frank predicated that he was going to get very far with his profession and he was right, as Terry Wogan went on to become one of Britain's top radio and television presenters and was knighted by the Queen of England. Terry Prone, meanwhile went on to become part of Carr Communications before starting her own company The Communications Clinic.

As the midnight oil burnt rapidly at Amalgamated Artistes on Dublin's famous Kildare Street, the directors became frantic over the continuing slow sales of tickets when a bombshell hit with the news that violence was escalating in Northern Ireland, which had a ripple effect on the Capital City of the Irish Republic! People became very nervous, least of all Frank Bailey. He made frantic telephone calls to a film/television director in London who was later to become closely aligned with the popular TV programmes 'Porridge' and 'Last of the Summer Wine'. Frank suggested as an eleventh hour deal to bring in the ever popular Cliff Richard! He said that Pat Peterson could meet him upon arrival with some of the Irish stars at Dublin airport with lots of publicity! The director informed him that he wasn't sure if Cliff Richard was available, and secondly it would cost a fortune, "…and I would suggest Frank," he continued, "that you should sell the shirt off your back, if you want this project to succeed!" The well-meant effort was binned by his co-directors. The mood was sombre but extremely anxious. The show must go on!

The night before the event, Frank aggressively said to me, "You cannot wear black shoes with a white suit on stage!" A friend of mine painted the shoes silver and so on the 20th August 1969, I was to take to the stage as host of 'Pop in the Sun' at the National Stadium in Dublin. The tension was high. We all gathered backstage and most people knew each other; with the lovely Muriel Day, who had represented Ireland that year in the Eurovision Song Contest in Madrid, taking centre stage. One famous singer of the day was overheard saying "This damn thing is run by faggots and fruits, with a queer compere to booth!" The remarks were passed on to Frank Bailey who immediately came down from the gantry and ordered the singer out of the premises. The singer was never employed again and lost a very successful career!

One of the headline acts was the beautiful songsters, the folk group from Donegal, The Emmet Spiceland. They all wished me luck as host of the show but I particularly remember Donal Lunny of the group saying to me "Good luck man, you have a big night ahead of you!"

Muriel Day, our first female entrant into the Eurovision Song Contest, was like a mother to me! We had met a month earlier in Jury's Hotel and I remember her saying to me, "Sweetheart if you haven't got nerves you wouldn't be human!"

I had been informed that there were two minutes to go, and so a stagehand brought me to the top the stairs which ran all the way down into the arena. I noticed that the place was half full but I had a job to do and I wasn't going to disappoint. I was introduced to much fanfare as the spotlights searched the audience, eventually blinding me as I came into focus. I received a rapturous applause as I threw the red cape off onto the beautifully designed set by Gavin Duffy. The show went without a hitch and the audience loved it, with all credit to our director Frank Bailey. When the lights dimmed and the show was over, my mother who accompanied me everywhere joined us all for a meal in the Trocadero restaurant but Frank Bailey was nowhere to be seen. I was informed that he was 'gutted' at the poor sales performance. The next day's press reviews said that I was a genial host who co-ordinated a well-produced show but it lacked an audience! Shay Healy writing in *Spotlight Magazine* gave it the title 'Flop in the Sun!' Frank Bailey went ballistic and if that wasn't bad enough Alan Gibson had underwritten the show and had to pay all of the debts! Frank said to me, "It's not your problem, dear heart, you did me proud at the Stadium."

As the weeks followed I continued as his Personal Assistant but to be elevated as Administration Assistant on his plays 'Part of the Main' starring Hollywood actor O.Z. Whitehead. He then suggested that I tour the Dublin region with a show called 'Opportunity Knocks for You'. John O'Sullivan of John & Olivia fame from the TV Show 'Like Now' directed by Bill Keating was taken on board along with a secretary. It was exceedingly hard work and none of us were paid for it. It was frustrating, and so by early October 1970 I told him that I was leaving. I remember him telling me enthusiastically that his plans were underway to bring modern theatre to the western regions of Ireland with the great Irish actor Peter O'Toole. I wished him well and we parted company on good terms. I was never to see him again. The troubles in Northern Ireland were about to ignite which attracted worldwide attention, and tourism in the Republic of Ireland was greatly affected. Whatever about the Capital City, Dublin, the west of Ireland was to suffer greatly and so was the idealism of Frank J. Bailey who was found dead in Galway some months later. A legend had passed on and as a young man his death affected me greatly.

I was very proud that the 'National University of Ireland Galway' in its new €6 million arts wing and cultural centre, named a wing in the memory of the late Frank J. Bailey. He was a man of great vision and a great loss to Irish Theatre and the entertainment industry as a whole! I am privileged to have been his friend.

THREE

Escape to Foreign Shores!
The Agony and Ecstasy of being Gay!

The lights had faded, the curtain had fallen, the birds had flown their nest and Amalgamated Artistes was no more! It was a depressing time and one of disillusionment for a young eighteen year old as I felt like I was carrying Christ Church Cathedral on my shoulders! I decided to go and try my hand in Toronto, Canada where my Aunt Ethel and her husband lived with their children. In those days in winter I had to fly Dublin-Shannon-New York-Toronto. When I reached New York I was in awe of this famous city and I couldn't comprehend the idea of living in it as it was so fast and impersonal. I was greeted in Toronto by my Aunt Ethel and her husband and we left for their home to meet with my cousins. The following day I was taken to see Lake Ontario which forms part of the five great lakes of North America and Canada. Later in the day it was off to visit more relatives, with the younger ones asking question after question about my life in show business.

The Dominicans were always protective of me and gave me the name of a French/Canadian priest, Father La Blanc O. P. who lived in Hamilton, Canada, and so on another day I took the train *(which was to become one of many)* to meet the man himself. He was a theologian and a visionary spirit for Canada, and tried to persuade me to take up citizenship and live and study in Hamilton and join the Dominicans. I always enjoyed his company and on each visit we would have Kentucky Fried Chicken in the snow! Our meetings were nuggets of great inspiration and I enjoyed his company immensely.

However, I declined the invitation and went in search of an agent with my portfolio in hand. I wanted to do radio as I had been complimented many times on my speaking voice and had tried Radio Eireann, with Terry Prone, telling me to keep knocking on the door! In Canada, I went from one to the other and eventually came across a man who was considered a 'big noise' in Toronto. He was a grotesque very large individual with whom I auditioned. He said he had a radio station that would snap me up in no time with a fine Irish speaking accent! I was impressed. We went into studio and recorded a demo which he was delighted with and said that he was meeting with the Head of Light Entertainment, of the Radio Station, and I should join them.

We drove for miles in his heated Chevrolet through thick and blistery snow until we eventually arrived at this large log cabin. He came out to greet us, a man with a long beard like a hippy and invited us in. When we entered there were six couples, all teenage boys, to whom I was introduced. I was handed a beer but declined and asked for water to which our host replied, "God, darn! Who drinks water these days? I thought all you Irish drank like fishes!" To be sociable I took the beer and to my embarrassment he played the demo for his guests who loved it! One beer followed another and so he offered me some whiskey to which I declined. He invited me into another room with the agent to discuss 'business' regarding the demo tape as I thought! When we entered the room it was his bedroom with a massive bed adorned with bear rugs! "My friend and I want to get to know you better!" he said lustfully. "I can make you a big star, so why don't you strip off and the boys outside will join us later!" I was petrified and asked the agent to take me home which he did with remorse. We drove all the way back in silence without even saying 'goodnight' to each other!

I was totally at a loss as to what to do next and so I got a job with an English stationer's company selling carbon paper on the phone! It was soul destroying and the English boss hated the Irish with a vengeance and so I was the subject of constant bullying. The weather was extremely cold, I couldn't stand it and so I left Canada for Chicago, flying onwards to Wichita Falls and into Oklahoma City where my Aunt Evelyn and Sarah lived with their families. The air, grace and sunshine were a warm welcome from the deep snow and cold of Canada. The welcome I received was beyond reproach!

The taste of the United States was appealing and the history of the Native American people was both disturbing and intriguing. I could identify with them as a marginalised community!

I had begun writing at an early age and had written many un-published stories including a novel. As a result I went around schools and colleges, reading for the students. I was invited onto an American television chat show in Oklahoma City and did some radio work as well. As a result, a certain female opera singer Kris took an interest and asked me out! I used to cycle to her house and then get into her car and we would go for a trip around Lake Overholser for chit chat! I had to suppress my sexuality which was frustrating. She was very religious and didn't believe in sex before marriage plus she didn't like 'Fruits!' I asked her what were fruits and she replied 'Homosexuals!'

I was walking on thin ice which I certainly didn't like. I made excuse after excuse not to see her until she telephoned my Aunt Sarah saying that she needed to see me urgently as it was regarding an invitation to the White House! I reluctantly agreed to see her and there it was, an invitation to sing in front of President Nixon! She asked me to accompany her but I had no alternative but to refuse as my visa would have expired by then and I would be back in Ireland. I am a home bird at heart and the old sod was calling me back. I missed my beloved mother tremendously although we spoke by phone every ten days. We hadn't a telephone at home and so my mother would go to the Dominican Convent where the nuns were delighted to be of service. I remember one of the mad sisters getting online and saying to me; "Hiya! Yankee Doodle Dandy!"

The time arrived for me to leave on July 3rd 1971, the eve of American Independence Day, and on the way to the airport the highway was full of billboards advertising the arrival of Bob Hope for the big Day. I got to the airport and sadly said goodbye to my family and flew from Oklahoma City to Dulles Airport in Washington DC and onwards to New York's JFK.

When I got to New York I was met by my former college friend, Austin Fogarty, who was jobbing for the summer in New York City accompanied by his delightful aunt who was a nun and had been working in New York for many years. After the brief meeting in the coffee lounge I boarded the new Aer Lingus 747 'St. Patrick', bound for Shannon and Dublin. The same aircraft was to carry the future Pope John Paul II on his historic visit to Ireland in 1979. I was saddened to leave the United States but I was to return many times later. It was one of the most enjoyable flights of my life, apart from the flight Tony and I made from Perth, Australia to Bangkok in 1989.

The majestic St. Patrick touched down on time at Dublin airport and there to greet me were my mother and father, my sisters, my grandmother Lambe and Ledwidge, my aunts, uncles and friends. It was a big event in those days to travel home from the North American continent as if we had flown from space! However I was exceedingly grateful and the sight of my beautiful glamorous mother warmed the cockles of my heart! I loved her so much. She had knitted six jumpers, all laid out on my bed when I got home.

After a few days my father said to me that it was time to settle down, get a job and before long I would be married to a good woman! I was physically sick! I got a job with Irish Life Assurance Company, bought a car and my Uncle Noel would take me up to the Phoenix Park on a Sunday morning for driving lessons. On the side roads he would scream at me, "Look now, you've just killed 15 people!" There was no-one in sight and he drove me crazy! I love my Uncle Noel to bits but in those days he nearly gave me a nervous breakdown! After a tumultuous time in Dublin and the attitude of the church, plus a crisis of conscience, I left for London which was nearly my demise! I met a semi-professional footballer who was bisexual and we were mad about each other. He took me to the Café Royal and introduced me to the then Prime Minister, Ted Heath, at a sports event.

However he refused to go into gay bars as London was swinging in those days and he was paranoid at what people might think. I was so enthralled by him, I brought my mother and young sister Denise, over from Dublin to meet him. We all went to the London Palladium to see Bruce Forsyth, and the following day we went to Brighton Beach where he cut his foot and bled profusely whilst my mother bandaged it until we got him to the local hospital. He was a fine looking man, and within a week he was back on the pitch. He used to say to me *"Lee, every goal I score is for you, my love!"* My heart would melt! However he was extremely scared of people finding out that he was bi-sexual, although whilst he was with me he was very gay! One night we were at Lord's cricket ground when he met an old friend who said, "C' blimey mate don't tell me you are batting for the other side!" he was mortified. Christmas 1973, I had to return to my family in Dublin and so he drove me early morning to Heathrow Airport where he presented me with a bloodstone ring.

After the Christmas break I returned to London expecting to be picked up by him but he never arrived. I tried frantically to contact him over several days but there was no response. It was the first time in my life that my heart was broken! I was left alone and isolated, I was an empty soul and so I attempted the un-imaginable by taking an overdose of pills swallowed down by a bottle of gin! There was nothing further from my upbringing that would constitute such a stupid act!

I woke up several days later in the Royal Free Hospital with my lover standing over me. I was so groggy and parching with thirst and he said to me, "Lee, I'm sorry but I cannot continue!" I never responded and he left, never to be seen again. I knew instinctively that it was over and I was more concerned about getting healthy and so within a few days I was ready to leave the hospital feeling very tired and depressed. I knew by then that it was certainly not love but rather infatuation.

I returned home to Dublin yet again but it wasn't all plain sailing as I went from the frying pan into the fire! My father, on hearing that I was gay and my attempted suicide, went ballistic! My mother intervened saying, "At least my son doesn't dress up in women's clothes!" To which came the retort, "What is that supposed to mean?" "Take your uncle who prances around the stage every Christmas as a panto dame, and I honestly believe he dresses up in that house in Drumcondra; or your other uncle when he came out of the religious order, he went to live in the gay capital of Britain, Brighton!" My father was speechless and walked out of the house straight to the pub! My mother said to me, "Take what you need for a few nights, you're going to stay with your grandmother! When I got to my Nanny Lambe's, she hugged and kissed me as she knew that I was gay and so did all of my aunts and uncles who never had a problem with it.

It was a terrible time, a time of confusion and perplexing anxiety and that is why my heart goes out to young people today who may find themselves in similar circumstances. We must always remember that homophobia is still alive and well in the 21st Century! However back then the demons were at war in my head 'Why wasn't I born straight? Why could I not settle down with a woman and have children?' I felt like a disgrace and useless whilst others taunted me over my sexuality; it was a no-win situation and my enthusiasm had hit rock bottom. I sat down and read Rose Kennedy's autobiography (mother of JFK) *Times to Remember* and this book gave me the motivation to pick myself up, brush myself down and start all over again!

FOUR

My First and Only Love
25 Years!

It was summer of 1974, when I picked up my old friend Tom Waters, and drove to Stephen's Green to park the car. Tom wanted me to see this gay bar 'Rice's on the Green. They were mostly elderly gay men in the front lounge whilst the back was occupied by students from the College of Surgeons. It was a friendly welcoming bar run by the family and there was never any animosity towards the gay community. Tom then suggested that we go down the street to the famous Bartley Dunne's, when a shiver ran down my spine! "Whatever is the matter with you?" he asked. I informed him what Frank Bailey had said years earlier but he dismissed it out of hand, saying "I've never heard so much rubbish! We are going!"

We walked down the street past the old Mercer hospital where I had gone years earlier with my mother about my alleged flat foot! When we arrived at the door there were two well-dressed gentlemen (Barry & Gerry Dunne). They greeted us and we walked into this dimly-lit bar with portraits of Hollywood stars, candlelit tables romantically finished off with a stock of international drinks behind the bar, all very French in style. Delightful!

We ordered our drinks and stood by the wall as we were eyed from head to toe from other curious customers! As the crowds began to arrive I noticed this familiar face staring at me but paid no attention. Tom excused himself to go to the bathroom and the staring continued almost to a point of being uncomfortable! Then I noticed Tom chatting to him and coming back with two drinks and saying that the guy over there bought us these two drinks and he says "thanks!" "Thanks for what I asked?"

He startled me with his reply, "The Honda 50." I suddenly realised that he was the disc jockey from Butlins to whom I awarded the prize back in 1969. I went over to thank him and he asked me to take a seat and so I did. (Tom was chatting up someone else.) I asked him if he enjoyed the ride! "I beg your pardon?" he asked. "The Honda 50" I replied. "No, I sold it," he said.

I later found out that he was in fact Tony Keogan, from Rialto, and he was an only child who lived with his elderly parents who were very religious. I said, "Listen mate, with all due respects, I don't want to get involved with religious hang-ups!" He went white in the face! He thought I was leaving but I was only adjusting the chair. He placed his hand on my knee and said, "Please don't go!"

"I'm not going anywhere, I'm just adjusting the chair although I should be going as I'm driving."

"Please stay, I've thought of you for years, the night you walked into Butlins, my legs were like jelly!"

"No kidding mate, so were mine, but I was suffering with a toothache!"

"It wasn't noticeable," he said. "I saw you staring and I thought you were trying to win the popular vote! It didn't work by the way, as you were very good. Fair is fair!"

I bought us both a drink and the conversation continued with me thinking of my car parked on

Stephen's Green. He was so interested, I got nervous after my past history with men and so I excused myself to go to the bathroom. I could feel myself wobbling and knew that I wasn't capable of driving! When I returned he was about to order another drink but I refused saying I needed air and something to eat. He suggested a 'burger joint' around the corner on Aungier Street. I agreed.

We exited Bartley Dunne's and turned left up the darkened Digges Lane and halfway up he took hold of my hand and I fell into his arms caressing and kissing each other like young teenagers! We then continued up the lane onto Bow Lane East and unbeknownst to us the laneway was to be our home in less than ten years and become internationally famous as the home of *INCOGNITO!* We went into the burger restaurant and chatted endlessly as we stared each other in the eye! This was no ordinary stare as he didn't seem like a one-night stand and he was deadly serious.

We left the restaurant with intentions of sharing a taxi to our respective homes. However, every taxi that was driving up and down he said, "Don't get that one." He then pulled me into a secluded spot and professed his undying love for me and said, "If I could marry you, I would do it in a second!" This guy was serious and so was I! He got on his knees and said, "Will you be my boyfriend? My Queen forever?"

I looked down upon this beautiful soul and thinking to myself 'I love the dramatics!' I replied, "Arise Sir Anthony, I accept." We were both over the moon but it was too soon to leave each other and so I telephoned a friend of mine who was a night manager in a popular Dublin hotel and asked if he had any spare rooms and he told me to come along immediately, which we did. When he heard the news of our engagement he gave us a Master Suite as a present.

It was June 16th 1974, and the relationship lasted a quarter of a century! It was a beautiful and exhilarating romance, so much different from my time with the footballer! Tony had no hang-ups, he was into John Lennon, Mike Oldfield amongst others; he was a beautiful soul and we jelled perfectly well together. I was so thrilled that God at last had sent me a decent soul, a man of love and trust and an all-round nice guy! In hindsight and looking back we had no idea that we would settle in that area or even become pioneers of the Irish Gay Commercial scene, as radical as it might have been!

We went to the hotel and had a night of heavenly passion without sleep! As dawn approached I knew that Tony had to be in work by 8pm as he worked with the ESB on Fitzwilliam Street and so I offered to take him back to Rialto for a change of clothes and pick him up and drop him into Fitzwilliam Street. He reluctantly agreed as he wanted to take the day off! We went down to the reception at 5.30am and my friend was aghast that we were leaving so early! I told him the circumstances and he said the room was free again that night if we wanted to stay, with his compliments. There was no need to ask Tony, as he was already heading for the lift! We went back to our suite and slept like babies!

When we awoke we showered and went back to our respective homes for a change of clothing and I told him to bring his work clothes for the following morning.

When I arrived home my mother knew instinctively that something good had occurred and I told her. She was over the moon! "When am I going to meet him?" she asked. "The weekend I hope." She was delighted. I eventually picked Tony up and we headed back to the hotel.

When I went to get the key the receptionist said, "Mr Ledwidge, would you like your dinner in the room or in the restaurant?" I replied that I hadn't ordered dinner! "Dinner is allowed with two bottles of wine with the compliments of the hotel!" I was taken aback but delighted! The Manager was allowed into our clubs free of charge until he left for New Zealand to start a new life some years later.

As we had nowhere to stay after the hotel it was going to be difficult to find accommodation, and our dear late friend, Vincent Hanley, who was a rising star in RTE offered to put us up on the odd weekend at his place in Terenure.

We eventually got our own apartment in Dartmouth Square in Ranelagh, Dublin 6, which was within walking distance of the city. The night arrived for Tony to meet my mother and she was attending a dinner-dance at the CIE in Inchicore. Tony was very nervous but my mother entered the lounge in a long salmon flowing dress looking stunning and she threw her arms around him, as if she had known him all her life.

Tony was chuffed and couldn't get over how youthful and glamorous she was. She brought all of her friends out of the dining area to introduce her son's boyfriend. This was a remarkable achievement for 1974. She assured him of her full support and wished us both well for the future! She invited him up to our home for dinner; however, I still had the task of telling my father! The meeting with my mother went very well indeed and we were both very pleased and so it was off to Bartley Dunne's to celebrate.

It was time for me to tell or challenge my father and so when the time came I went to see him and said, "Dad, I don't care whether you like it or not but I'm gay and I have met a boyfriend!" I was expecting an ear-bashing but to my surprise he said, "Congratulations son, you're telling me something that I already know, but I wanted you to tell me yourself. Bring Tony up to our house for dinner soon!" I replied that the invitation was already extended!

"What?" he replied. "Why is it that I'm the last one in this house to know anything?"

"Because you're never around Dad!" I said.

"Look who's talking! I never know where you are!" I looked at him and laughed. "One of the mysteries of life! Ha! Ha!"

"Get out and don't forget to bring that young man up, I'll want to ask him a few questions!"

"You'll do no such thing," I replied and I was on my way to convey the good news.

Times were swinging, life was good and everything looked bright on the horizon, Tony and I went to see Mam and Dad and we had a beautiful dinner with drinks afterwards. My father and Tony hit it off very well and were friends up until his death in November 1993. Both my grandmothers loved Tony as did all of my aunts, uncles and cousins! My grandmother Lambe took a particular liking to him, after all he was the boyfriend of her eldest grandchild! She loved him dearly and he in turn adored her. It was acutely recognised by my entire family that Tony was an only child with elderly conservative catholic parents, who wouldn't have been as liberal as my family, and so Tony became part of the family. It was a great source of comfort to me to which I will always be eternally grateful. Tony then invited me to have tea in their home in Rialto, and I was more scared of this than running down the steps at the National Stadium on August 20th 1969!

I arrived at the house on New Ireland Road and I was brought into the parlour and sat down. Mrs Keogan entered with a tray of tea and biscuits and politely said "hello". I was as nervous as hell as both parents had sent Tony to a psychologist whom they thought would cure his 'homosexuality' and here I was the 'devil' in the room or so I thought! I immediately stood up. "Sit down young man, my name is Nora and although I don't approve of what is going on at the moment, I want to give you both my blessings and I want you both to be happy. If it's God's will, who am I to stand in his way?"

She went on talking about Weaver Square School where Tony *(she called him Anthony)* went to school, the same school that I had attended. She spoke highly of the nuns. As I was beginning to breathe again his father walked in, pipe in hand, cap on head and said, "Anthony, make sure that young man gets home safely!"

"No problem there, Dad, he lives with me!"

"Good god, what is the world coming to?" Jim Keogan was ultra-conservative, a staunch Roman Catholic from County Cavan, with some republican views. As the years passed he mellowed towards me until we became best friends!

The time had come for us to leave and we politely said goodbye to each other. I was glad to get out into the air and I said to Tony, "This is going to be a rocky ride!" However we were madly in love with one another and nothing was going to get in our way! By Christmas time my parents had invited Tony's parents to dinner but Jim refused to go. Nora arrived and received a warm welcome and had several glasses of sherry! A lady unaccustomed to drinking, she bent the rules for Christmas Day, and was in top form! Although she had been sick most of her life after the birth of Tony, Nora loved her fashion and jewellery and both his parents were good honest souls of which I admired. She lived for another fourteen years and it was a privilege to have been part of her life as her son's partner. She was truly a Christian woman!

FIVE

'Studio One'
Ireland's 'First Gay Commercial Night Club'
5th December 1975

In my view the love between two men is as natural as the love a man has for a woman. We should never tag ourselves with gender identities but when two souls are attracted to each other no man has the right to pull asunder! Tony and I were like two peas in a pod and settled into married life as sure as night follows day.

In those early days of conservatism in our liberated life, Tony would often comment that all we were short of was a piece of paper to recognise our relationship, but that didn't matter as equal marriage would never come in our lifetime, and unfortunately he was right as it never came in his lifetime! We were extremely proud of each other and dressed like rock 'n' roll kids; or suits, shirt and ties whenever the occasion arose. We received a lot of respect and we gave the same in return. We were the wind beneath each other's wings and this continued unabated for many years.

People admired us for our courage but there were those within the gay community who hated us because we were popular! The gay community can at times be very bitchy but we gave as much as we got. Gay people can be very fickle and insecure, but in hindsight I can see similar traits in straight people. There is nothing worse than a jealous wife or a cheating husband! It's all part of the makeup of the human psyche that makes the world revolve. I am as guilty of that as anyone else!

We enjoyed each other's work ethics; we had the same political views and knew various politicians who believed in what we were doing. We were singing from the same hymn sheet and believed that one day gay life would be recognised and we were right. It was through my association with the Church that we also knew some senior church personnel who were of the belief that we were living through history, but never in my wildest dreams did I think that so many clergy would become members of our future club; neither did we ever realise that a Roman Catholic priest would drop dead in our club in 1994, catapulting us into world news headlines!

In 1975, I was asked to host a show with the late great Cecil Sheridan, star of variety shows and pantomimes along with the great tenor, Edmund Browne, and Sonny Knowles who was a friend of my family. Tony saw me in action and said later that he felt twelve feet tall! Later that night we went to a night club and joined up with some friends, including the manager of a famous cinema who introduced us to a guy he had met who was a budding disc-jockey and later went on to become a radio talk show host!

On that night, Tony suggested that we open a night club and so we discussed it. He always shunned the limelight but nevertheless we agreed and acquired the basement and first-floor back room at 37 North Great Georges Street, in Dublin. It was with the help of many friends we painted, decorated and set out the first gay commercial night club in Ireland on December 5th 1975. We were nervous but positive!

Many of the show business fraternity of the day, along with politicians and gay people who are household names today, attended. All of my old friends from stage, theatre and the press were in attendance, including Tom Hennegan, of the *Evening Herald*, and a man I was tipped off to look out for was Terry O'Sullivan, of the *Evening Press*, who was fond of a drink and who would have a mistress in tow! We weren't left waiting as Terry walked in, true to form, and we immediately clicked. Terry was to give us publicity in his column *Dubliner's Diary* for some time to come and unbeknownst to us his daughter, Nuala O'Faolain, was to do the same as an *Irish Times* journalist in less than two decades later.

In those days, as you can imagine, we hadn't got the social media that we have today; there were no mobile phones and unless you had a landline you would spend ages on a queue to use the public telephone hoping it would work, or banging endlessly on the 'A' button to communicate! When I tell my niece of these stories today, she tells me that I was living in the Stone Age! They were tough but challenging times and we took nothing for granted.

Meanwhile, back at the club, I was always fascinated by the professions of customers who frequented our establishment and in those early days they came from all corners of Ireland and abroad. One leading personality who referred to North Great Georges Street as *"a city dump"* had no problem buying a property there some years later. We had a guy from London one night accompanied by an elderly lady whose surname was Bowes Lyon and claimed to be a cousin of the Queen of England! Whether that story was true or not she most certainly was very regal and eloquent, with a vast knowledge of the royal family and British history that fascinated us!

On another occasion we had a guy who claimed Irish heritage and was a former member of the CIA and was on duty in Dallas, Texas, the day President John Fitzgerald Kennedy was assassinated on November 22nd 1963. He turned out to be a fruit seller from the East End of London and was wanted by the British Police!

A leading member of the Fianna Fail, ruling government party of the day, didn't care where he frequented but he was a nightly visitor to our club who offered us £200 to perform in front of him which disgusted us. The same man would host private meetings of his party including its leader at his D4 home. One night at a party there, I fell asleep to be awoken by Tony, shouting, "Let's get out of here" and as I awoke in a daze our friend was on the floor with a black eye having tried to molest me in a drunken state!

However my grandmother Ledwidge began to disapprove of our relationship as she wanted me to pursue my career in radio and possibly television because at one time I nearly made it into RTE *(Irish Radio and Television)* but because of a strike, my love and ambitions for Tony overruled my decision in pursuing that notion. I gave up the idea and he in turn gave up a job with the ESB so that we could concentrate on each other and our careers. It was without doubt a leap into the dark! My grandmother Lambe disagreed entirely and believed that if we loved each other we could countenance any problems and continue, which we did. Whatever my grandmother Lambe said I adhered to. I adored my grandmother, the mother of eleven children and I as her eldest grandchild, had a special place in her heart. I wear her wedding ring to this day. In turn I loved my mother exceedingly and I was in awe of her until she died in my presence.

LGBTQ people need the support of their families and friends, similar to what I got back in the 1970s and beyond, but never expect miracles even in this day of the 21st Century where we have equal marriage. I cannot tell you enough the amount of anxiety and mental pressures our customers went through in the latter half of the 1970s and beyond as we became aware of their insecurities for being gay; people were thrown out of their homes, violated and molested by family members and in some cases people took their own lives rather than face the consequences. I remember being personally upset upon hearing the news that a young chap had committed suicide who was a regular visitor to our club, and his boyfriend did the same thing a week later. People would call them names and refer to them as Hansel & Gretel which led them to take their own lives. They had been perplexed and confused over their sexuality; the non-conformation of the law and society's attitudes towards them for being gay and being themselves led them into that fatal mistake. I have always maintained that it was a form of bullying that led them to make that ultimate decision.

I remember going to my grandmother Lambe and telling her how I felt at the devastating news and she asked me to go around to the church and light two candles for their souls. I entered the church, Our Lady of Good Council, where I was baptised, and lit the two candles and sat in silence in the empty church, totally void of any emotion and asked God what it was all about? The serenity of this sacred ground gave me no answers but perhaps a sense of peace, and so I went back to Tony and told him of my experience but he dismissed it out of hand saying there was no God! I was greatly disturbed.

However, that aside we went with our fledgling club with both gay men and women in attendance from all walks of life, and each night brought new challenges! Some guys didn't know if they were 'Arthur or Martha' but it was all part of the growing mechanism within the human spirit. I remember the first transvestite coming into the club with her make-up all over the place and I politely said, "You need to do something about your slap dear," and she was horrified! As I have already said, I lived in London in the early 1970s and saw how they honed it to perfection.

One evening, Tony came running to the reception, full of anxiety regarding a special customer paying into the club who was a popular drag artiste! Tony said that the entertainer was more than amused to be charged in as he frequently went to night clubs without having to pay in! I replied sarcastically, "How times have changed!" In walked a well-groomed man, "Hello dear, I'm Alan Amsby aka Mr Pussy!" We both looked each other in the eye, burst out laughing and greeted each other accordingly. We had clicked and were to remain friends and become business partners eventually.

Alan, was always known as 'Ireland's Leading Misleading Lady,' Mr Pussy! He was a very funny man who had a room in a corporation house in Finglas, North Dublin with a beautiful and generous woman, Essie and her family. Essie was the traditional Irish 'Mammy' who cooked, cleaned and looked after everyone in her flock with the caring maternal love given by any mother to her children. Tony and I developed a very special bond with Essie and I always remember her and her family with great fondness.

In hindsight looking back, the years were both challenging and exciting, but for some it was a lonely existence born out of fear, anxiety and frustration because of their sexual orientation. I remember one guy telling us that when he awoke on a Monday morning he would count the days waiting for the weekend so that he could be with his own in our club! The atmosphere and the mingling with other gays gave him hope but the anxiety and frustration came when he went into work on a Monday morning, not being able to tell his work colleagues where he had spent the weekend or discuss his lifestyle with family or friends. He was living in an oppressive society bearing the fruits of the unknown as to what lay ahead in the future.

Six

Ireland's Leading Misleading Lady!
That's for Sure!

In the early part of 1976, Studio One was attracting more customers than we cared to think about and some were very undesirable individuals, so we began to weed them out. Alan, Tony and I would frequently go to the 'Coffee Dock' at Jury's hotel in Ballsbridge after we finished work. We also frequented the 'Bombay' on Richmond Street or Lord John's *(off O'Connell Street)* and although these establishments were not gay, they were gay-friendly as was Zhivago in Baggot Street or Sloopy's in Fleet Street. We were also theatre goers and loved the theatre which was a great outlet from our everyday lives. One night at a club in Leeson Street a guy made disparaging remarks regarding our sexuality when Shay Healy came to the rescue with the involvement of the management. The individual was asked to leave the club but threatened us on the way out, resulting in us having to be escorted out sometime later by bouncers and into a taxi to take us home a short distance away.

Alan was anxious to come into business with us and so we agreed, but he was not everyone's cup of tea as some very influential people came to us saying it would be the greatest mistake of our lives and that 'Pussy' was 'False' like his 'Alter Ego' and a 'User-Controller' and it wasn't long before we were named as 'Pussy's Kittens' a name we disliked intensely. We were fascinated with this man of the world who seemed to know it all!

We went to our solicitors and formed the company known as 'Mr Pussy's Nite Club Limited' with the three of us as directors/shareholders. We revamped Studio One and on Sunday night 27 June 1976, 'Mr Pussy's Nite Club' was born at 37 North Great Georges Street, with PR working at full speed resulting in a lot of publicity. Once again the stars and the press turned out side-by-side with the gay community to celebrate another new venture. Alan performed as 'Mr Pussy' that night and it has always fascinated me the way he put the make-up, wig and costume together. He was meticulous about the wig, having worked for wig creation in London and his make-up was faultlessly crafted to suit his attire. There was no doubt about it he was a 'Master' of his craft. The attention to detail was done to perfection with the sequence of his gown right down to his nylon stockings and high heels that would have left some women standing in awe, and they did!

Alan was a very funny guy and as we say in Ireland 'the craic was ninety!' One night a guy exposed himself to us and Alan retorted, "O' my God I've seen a bigger woodbine!" On another occasion a guy jumped out in front of us at four in the morning in London's West End with a knife in his hand and shouted, "Give me your money! I'm Jack the Ripper!" To which Alan replied "Get you dear! I'm Pussy the stripper!" Jack the so-called Ripper fled the scene looking bemused!

On another occasion at a country gig only a couple of people turned up and when he went to get paid, the manager informed him that there was no money! Alan insisted that he was promised 'half of the door' to which the manager quipped, "Which half would you like?" It is true to say that he was a pioneering drag act in Ireland who toured the country playing in hotels to dingy pubs but he was a good old trooper. He always ensured as much as possible to get back to the club before early morning closing where fun and frolics went on all night! I laughed quietly to myself recently when he published a book, acknowledging everyone and anyone, but the people who cared and looked after him as he struggled through life were not acknowledged. It didn't go un-noticed as one observer said, "What do you expect from a man like him?"

Meanwhile a cabaret venue called 'The Fiesta' opened on Dublin's Talbot Street, less than ten minutes' walk from our club, starring some of the world's greatest stars, Johnny Ray, Ruby Murray to name but a few, including acts from Las Vegas who visited our club regularly. Johnny Ray came around every night during his tenure and the day before he departed to appear at the Royal Variety Command Performance in front of Her Majesty the late Queen Mother at the London Palladium, he invited Tony, Alan and I to his suite at the Gresham Hotel for drinks and a chat. It was one of the most memorable nights of my life as Johnny reflected on his incredible life and career.

Johnny Ray was an American singer/songwriter and pianist who was huge in the United States and around the world in the 1950s and '60s with hits like 'Cry' and 'The Little White Cloud That Cried' and 'Walkin' My Baby Back Home'. Tony Bennett called him the "Father of rock and roll" and even Elvis agreed with that statement. The Beatles admitted that during their fledgling careers they listened to Johnny Ray. He was given his own star on the Hollywood Walk of Fame, *6201 Hollywood Boulevard*. Today he will be remembered being featured in the video of Dexys Midnight Runners arriving at Heathrow Airport in 1952 with their hit single 'Come on Eileen'. He will also be remembered for his appearance in the major movie; *There's No Business Like Show Business* with Marilyn Monroe.

However back at his suite in the Gresham Hotel the bar was stocked with Black Tower wine which he loved and any other drink one could ask for! He spoke emotionally about his dear friend Judy Garland, star of the *Wizard of Oz* and he spoke of their 1969 European tour the year of her death in London. She was a great friend of Danny La Rue and frequented his club many times. It was a very poignant moment to hear it from the Master himself.

Johnny would often wear his cap and coat and leave the Gresham Hotel alone and walk across O'Connell Street to the GPO to look at the famous building associated with the 1916 Rising and the events that led to the creation of our nation as an independent Irish state. It was the scene of much fighting and where the Proclamation of Independence was read by Padraig Pearse. He seemed fascinated with Irish history.

One night I drove him to a club in Stillorgan with a large black carrier bag full of Black Tower wine. Johnny sailed in without a word from anyone and ordered the glasses and opener and sat there in the early morning hours drinking his beloved beverage. The management were only too glad to accommodate such a big star. In fairness he spent a fortune in our club and left us with memories to treasure. He worked right up until 1989, a year before his death at the Cedars Sinai Medical Centre in Los Angeles.

It was great pleasure for us to welcome another great star Ruby Murray into our club who had hit singles 'Heartbeat' along with 'Softly Softly' and in 1955, she had at least one single in the UK charts for 52 weeks. She was also the star of her own television show along with starring with Norman Wisdom at the London Palladium. Ruby's popularity led to her surname 'Murray' being adopted in Cockney rhyming slang as a rhyme for 'curry'. The reference to "having a curry tonight" appears in the BBC TV comedy series 'Only Fools and Horses'. Ruby was an affable lady and extremely interesting to talk to and one night sang 'Softly Softly' to us in the reception of our club.

Wayne Sleep, Royal Ballet dancer and choreographer, was another delightful visitor; a man full of interesting stories who later gained prominence by dancing with Princess Diana at the Royal Opera House in 1985. He was the subject guest on Eamon Andrews' 'This is Your Life' in 1981.

In 1977 we moved to Parnell Square three doors down from the Phoenix Club, run by the Irish Gay Rights Movement which was convenient for patrons to pop in and out! One day a Garda *(Police)* Superintendent asked if we were getting any trouble from anyone and I replied, "We must be the only clubs in the country with twenty-four hour Garda protection!" He looked perplexed until I reminded him that the Gardaí were outside 24/7 watching the comings and goings of people at the Sinn Fein HQ, which was up the street where it was believed IRA members would meet.

In the same year I drove with Tony and Alan to meet Alan's mum in London for the first time, and we hit it off straight away and I had a great affinity with her as she was a delightful and funny woman. So much so that she paid regular visits to Dublin to stay with my mum and dad, when on occasion we took her to my sister and her husband in Galway. My mum and my sister Denise went to stay with her in London in 1978. When his mother came over from London, my parents were left to look after her without any objections. My mother would take her to the Sports Club in Ballyfermot or the nearby Coldcut where she enjoyed herself. Alan, became much aligned with my family, from my grandmother Lambe and parents to my aunts and uncles, and he attended the weddings of my three sisters. He was always a guest at my parents' home for the annual Christmas dinner, he was one of the family. However twenty years later that friendship was strained when my family who had welcomed him into their lives and homes were abandoned. When it happened it was like reeling in the years and the story will be told in another chapter.

The bond between our families was now truly established. We acquired a German Shepherd dog and called him ALK (Amsby/Ledwidge/Keogan). He was a very loyal companion and when Mr Pussy's Nite Club ceased in 1980 my mother took him in and cared for his remaining years.

I have always been amused to hear that Elton John paid a visit to our club, but I have to dismiss this as idle gossip as he never did. He did however pay a visit to Flickers at the Hirschfield Centre in the 1980s which was run by the National Gay Federation.

It was never easy being gay in the 1970s, but as gay pioneering commercial businessmen we took derogatory remarks on the chin because we had no choice but to do so! The commercial aspect of the struggle helped in every way to spotlight and promote gay rights. However we were acutely aware of what our customers had to put up with in their jobs, family and social lives. Sometimes we were accused of going too far too quickly as some older people preferred to live as they were, but we couldn't and we wouldn't stop the progress we were making. We started having cabaret at the club every couple of Saturday nights and one young straight couple caught our eye; they were the extremely talented The Young Hoppers and the gay community loved them! In 2017, forty years later, Johnny Hopper, paid tribute to me for giving them their first break!

My glamourous Aunt Sadie *(Sarah)* paid us a visit from Oklahoma City in the United States of America who thought that Alan was the best thing since sliced bread! They danced the night away which continued right out onto Parnell Square at 4 in the morning! I was blessed to have had such a wonderful understanding family whose love sustained me through the years. 'The Pussy Years' had served their purpose, and so Tony and I furthered the business by leasing a property on Bow Lane East, off Aungier Street in Dublin 2, before purchasing it some years later. We were still friends with Alan and if the truth be known our friendship became stronger for many years to come!

SEVEN

The *INCOGNITO* Years
and The Death of a Priest

As we entered the arduous years of the 1980s we contrived an idea we had for a sauna club for gay men. This idea developed after visiting establishments in London, Paris, Amsterdam and Rome where they were popular and so *INCOGNITO* was created at 1–2 Bow Lane East, Dublin 2. We started out advertising it with GCN *(Gay Community News)*, *Pink Pages* in the UK and other publishing outlets including those in Northern Ireland. We went with a camp idea and appointed our dear friend, Jan in Belfast as our 'Lady Prime Minister for Northern Ireland Gay Issues'! George was an obese gay man of 25 years, from Leeds in the United Kingdom, who liked his cigars and brandy, and was christened 'Churchill' because of his attributes and drooling voice. He was a very funny individual and used to visit Tony and I in our club in the early 1980s. He was fascinated with Churchill and used to quote him with cigar and brandy in hand, "Success is not final, failure is not fatal: It is the courage to continue that counts." George moved to London with his job and used to promote the club amongst the gay scene there. Jackson in the west of Ireland was known as 'Minister for Rural Affairs'. The idea was to inform people outside of Dublin to be aware that the gay community in Ireland had the same facilities as other European States and it worked.

Tony and I worked endlessly at the club working up until 5am during the week and 9am at the weekends. It was extremely tough going! We created office and living space above the club, so in effect we were on the job 24/7. Our apartment became legendary for parties, meetings and debates! Alan Amsby held court many a night with our regular taxi company complaining that they would not continue picking him up at 5 or 6 in the morning whilst he kept them waiting, as one time they were left waiting for 45 minutes, as a drunken Mr Pussy finally gave into demands! The longer he stayed the longer we laughed, as Alan was extremely witty; but I always felt sorry for the poor taxi men and I have no doubt that Alan always charmed them in the end!

However, horrific dark clouds descended on the community in January 1982, with the brutal and savage murder of a regular patron of our night club, Charles Self. Charles worked as a set designer in RTE *(Irish Radio and Television)* and was renowned for his work on Ireland's longest running television chat show 'The Late Late Show' with Gay Byrne. He was an extremely likeable, well-versed and quiet gentleman who was savagely murdered at the home he shared with our friend top DJ Vincent Hanley in Monkstown, South Dublin. The murder was so callous that it shocked every reasonable individual on the island of Ireland and beyond. He had been stabbed 14 times. There was a slash wound to the throat, a piece of torn ligature around his neck, with the rest tied to a chair. The attack was so vicious that the stab wounds were 'through and through'. The weapon, an eight-inch kitchen knife with a white handle, had been wielded with such ferocity it had gone right through his body.

Tony and I along with his many friends attended a packed congregation at the service in St. Andrew's Presbyterian Church, Blackrock, prior to his remains been flown to Glasgow. I can still hear the cries of his dear aunt in the church to this day.

The gay community was turned upside down both north and south of the country as the Gardaí and the RUC *(Royal Ulster Constabulary)* used 'bulldog' tactics in their investigation 'outing' people who were gay, by storming into family homes, offices and factories in search of his killer. The sensitivity and unwarranted tactics left some people shell-shocked as families and employers enquired as to why the police were interested in them seeking a gay killer! Married men known to the police from frequenting gay establishments were interviewed, leaving them to face the consequences with their wives and children. There was a wave of people flying back into their 'closets' as a result. The relationship between the gay community and the police was seriously fractured. Sometime later, a senior member of the force told Tony and me privately that inexperienced officers had let the force down and there was some constructive work to be done in repairing that relationship. To this day the killer has never been found.

As 1982 rolled on, with the gay community totally despondent with the upset and lack of progress in catching this evil killer, another bombshell hit in September when a young man, Declan Flynn, was viciously attacked, beaten and killed in Fairview Park in Dublin. Declan, an employee of Aer Rianta at Dublin Airport, and a frequent visitor to our night club, was one of the most inoffensive people you could meet. He was a pleasant, quiet and mannerly person who wouldn't say boo to a goose! The homophobic murder was once again investigated by the Gardaí with far more professionalism than previously seen in the Charles Self killing, and five young men were arrested and charged. He had been badly beaten around the head and body and died at the scene.

Following the trial of the five men, they were freed on suspended sentences stirring an outcry from the gay community and the public at large with David Norris saying, "It could be interpreted as a licence to kill." As far as the gay community was concerned it was the straw that broke the camel's back and co-operation between the community and the Gardaí intensified for the better. There was greater understanding and a far more strategic approach was adopted on both sides which gave the community more confidence to trust them and we did. It was the start of *Gay Pride* marches each summer and *Pride* as it is now known attracts thousands of revellers on the streets of Dublin alone each year.

As the community struggled to get over the tragic devastation and loss of Charles and Declan, news was filtering through regarding a rare virus that was hitting gay men hard in the San Francisco area of the United States of America. As time went by, the gay capital of the world was joined by Southern California and New York, as chilling stories in the scurrilous press referred to it as the *Gay Plague*. HIV/AIDS had arrived big time and some public opinion looked unfavourably on the gay community. It was the lion that roared the loudest, setting the community backwards as we were beginning to make progress. It was an emergence that took everyone by surprise and then it got worse as men were dying like flies. If you contracted the disease you had a limited time left! It was horrifying! We heard through the grapevine that *Hollywood Legend* Rock Hudson was dying of HIV/AIDS and when he passed away on the 2nd October 1985, the world paid more attention to this deadly virus. Elizabeth Taylor, his friend, and co-star in the movie *Giant* went on to keep his memory alive by working tirelessly for AIDS charities and creating awareness of the disease. In Ireland, the UK and mainland Europe the virus had no boundaries and like a chilling wind on a turbulent ocean it arrived with ferocity. It was the saddest period in the history of the gay community ever.

In Ireland, protective measures were taken to educate the community with emphasis on safer sex but unfortunately it didn't stop many of my peers from dying. Funerals and graveyards were becoming common places and as the disease spread to the 'straight' community, Governments worldwide set out in a massive determined effort to find preventative measures to the killer disease; the virus was now a worldwide urgent concern.

If that wasn't bad enough, gay bashings were frequent in Dublin with a spate of incidents outside the *INCOGNITO* club, with Tony and me investing in high quality outside CCTV and a sting operation involving the Gardaí who eventually caught the culprits. There were many incidents when the laundry would be leaving our establishment and young guys would shout "Get the AIDS out of the bag!" Instead of being frightened or annoyed we were amused to receive a dead mouse in the post one day; to imagine some sick individual going to such lengths didn't bear thinking about.

We were also refused medical insurance because we were gay. Similarly, we were denied service at a 'straight' pub in the city centre after watching a movie at the cinema with the lame excuse that they only served 'couples', male and female! Patrons to our club would tell us of the horrific abuse and bullying they received in their workplace and another told us of how he was fifteen to twenty minutes late three times in a month for work because he was caring for his elderly father, and the boss used the excuse to fire him! Those were the dark, grim and bleary years of being gay during the AIDS epidemic in Ireland. I am not exaggerating when I say that people with homophobic attitudes were delighted and used this tragic excuse to bash gay people whenever the opportunity arose.

In 1986, I went to visit my aunts in Seattle, Los Angeles and Oklahoma City but whilst in the United States, I went to see for myself the situation in San Francisco. It was like the city of the walking dead! Apart from the warm welcome I received, I was encouraged to see the positivity of the gay community with a fighting unification of spirit singing their adoptive anthem 'We Will Overcome'. Three years later Tony and I did a tour of the United States calling into San Francisco to find that the situation was slightly improved. In January of the same year, we had been to Australia where the AIDS crisis was just as bad but the Aussies had a more direct approach without little drama and their Mardi Gras attracted thousands of revellers, both gay and straight, on the streets of Sydney that year. We met a lady in Melbourne who was eighty-five years of age who made pots of jam to sell in order to raise money for AIDS charities. She told us that her grandson (age 25) had the disease but she was confident that he would survive and her wish was to take him to Paris and dance under the Eifel tower on her ninetieth birthday!

On the 11th January 1988, Tony's beloved mother Nora died after a long illness. Tony's father Jim, my mum, Tony and I were with her on that chilly cold morning when she passed away. Apart from the sadness of her passing, it also turned out to be a miraculous day; after fourteen years of being his son's partner, Jim finally acceded and not only accepted our relationship but gave us his blessing as well.

In March of that year we took him to South Africa on a three weeks' holiday to see my two sisters, Yvonne and Denise who was living there at that time with her husband and young son. Yvonne and her husband Naren, a doctor and graduate of University College Galway, had been living there a number of years with their three children, and on that visit Tony became godfather to my niece Mitasha. Jim truly enjoyed the trip and one day went missing, and after a long search he was found chatting in a pub with the locals! Tony and I were extremely overworked that year and so we took a week's holiday in Mauritius, leaving Jim with my mum and the rest of the family in South Africa. Denise and her husband Derek returned with their son to live in Ireland some weeks later.

In April 1989, my beloved grandmother Lambe passed away and her death had a terrible effect on me. We had just returned from Australia and my mother was in South Africa when I started drinking to excess, landing myself in the Blackrock Clinic for a week. I woke up with baskets and bouquets of flowers thinking I was in a funeral parlour as gossip spread rapidly that I was dying of AIDS! I remember leaving the clinic and the doctor saying to me "You're the healthiest looking AIDS patient I've ever seen!"

It was cautiously back to the grindstone although still working marathon hours. The love, care and attention that Tony gave me was second to none! In 1990, we bought our first new home at Bridgewater Quay, ideally situated on the banks of the River Liffey in Dublin. We christened it the 'Nora Elizabeth Suite' named after Tony's mother and my grandmother Elizabeth Lambe, with marble plaques emblazoned with gold leaf on the front and balcony areas of the property. It was a palatial three-bedroomed home with chandeliers and bar in situ. We would from time to time let it out to top business executives, mostly from abroad but working in Ireland, and the famous Danny La Rue and his assistant Annie Galbraith stayed there during his tenure at the Olympia Theatre in 1992. My 40th birthday party was celebrated there with thirty guests for a three-course meal. There were many parties and meetings, some of which were very memorable and some I would prefer to forget about.

INCOGNITO attracted all kinds of people from all walks of life; it was a galaxy of professions spreading right across the board in Irish society. There were people in those days who are high-profiled personalities today who would literally 'freeze' at the idea of admitting they were gay, who offered no support for the LGBTQ community but privately have thanked the men and women of forty-odd years ago for our courage and determination. It was also a haven for international visitors, and some famous at that, who would retreat to the Irish capital city for relaxation. All of that was soon to change as *INCOGNITO* was about to be catapulted into world news headlines!

It was the middle of the night in November 1994, as I slept alone at home when the telephone rang; it was the manager of the *INCOGNITO* club, to tell me that Kevin had dropped dead and the emergency services were on their way. I knew immediately who 'Kevin' was. I dressed and left straight away for the city centre to be met by the Gardaí and a Garda Superintendent who was very sympathetic and understanding. I was briefed by the manager and the superintendent, of the circumstances that had just transpired. He asked me if I knew the gentleman who had died and I told him I had known him as a patron of the club, but this man was already in the public domain and his name was Father Liam Cosgrave, a member of the Montfort order in the parish of Baldoyle in North County Dublin. The superintendent said he was aware of the facts.

Father Liam Cosgrave was parish priest and his presbytery had been broken into and he had been threatened by a couple of thugs! The priest had gone to one of Ireland's Sunday newspapers *Sunday World* and reported the incident. A reporter and photographer were dispatched to Baldoyle where the priest laid bare his story and sat in full clerical regalia for his own photographic memorial and epitaph. It was like mana from heaven for news media here and around the world when he died to have such an edge on the story.

We were hounded by the national and international news media but I believe broadcaster, journalist and author John Farrell summed it up when he wrote: *"Thanks to the compassionate and dignified manner in which Liam tackled the hordes of hungry journalists who began stalking him around the clock, the situation reached a curious and unprecedented compromise: Father Cosgrave was spared the gross indignity of public censure. The Hierarchy, family members, friends, and devout members of his congregation may have found it difficult to accept, but they matured enough in the process to see that the good works Father Cosgrave had accomplished in his ministry could not be taken away from him, that the grateful memories of those he had helped could not be washed away or spoilt. For the first time it was tacitly acknowledged that being gay was not incompatible with moral virtue, that this 'moral disorder' did not preclude the possibility of genuine Christian love and witness.*

"Although much remains to be done, it was in great measure, Ledwidge's sympathetic reaching out to the bereaved that allowed his gay colleagues to mourn side by side with the members of his own congregation in an attitude of mutual acceptance and respect."

Some months later the *INCOGNITO* club was destroyed by fire, and a swarm of theories surfaced that it was the hand of God who destroyed it; others said it was the opposition and some said it was subversive organisations, but in actual fact it was accidental. The insurance company paid out and *INCOGNITO* was rebuilt and up and running again. There were a lot of people left with egg on their faces!

EIGHT

The Horse & Carriage
First Gay Bed & Breakfast in Ireland

Winners, Dublin Chamber of Commerce
Business Face Award 1993

In 1992, it was Tony's turn to enter hospital after excessive drinking and exhaustion. It was very rare that Tony got sick and my heart went out to him; after eighteen years we were still very much in love. Apart from the rows and tantrums we idolised each other and out of a wide ranging amount of friends Alan was very close as was our oldest friend Alex. Alan and I paid a visit to Alex's holiday home in Alicante, Spain, but before leaving Gatwick Airport where a storm was brewing, I telephoned Tony in Dublin to inform him of the situation and Alan asked to speak, telling him *"If this continues there will be no 'Ali' in Alicante tonight!"* Alan was petrified of flying in those days.

In the same year Danny La Rue did a week-long appearance at the Olympia Theatre and he stayed at our house in Bridgewater Quay. Tony, Alan and I attended the opening night and every other night I attended, greeting VIP guests on his behalf and taking them to greet him afterwards. Gay Byrne was very fond of Danny and interviewed him on his radio programme for one hour about his lifetime in show business. One hour wasn't enough, as one night we sat in the Trocadero

Restaurant until dawn as he reminisced about the stars he had met and worked with during his long illustrious career. During that week he ensured that my beloved mum had a box at the Olympia with her friends and he also paid a visit to our parental home to see my dad in the final year of his life.

At the beginning of 1993, the adjoining property to 1–2 Bow Lane East situated on the laneway facing onto 15 Aungier Street became available and so we took out a long lease and turned the property into a Bed & Breakfast and called it 'The Horse & Carriage'. We renovated and decorated the nine rooms, with a large breakfast and lounge area which also functioned for meetings, lectures, radio interviews and a couple of television interviews for an independent company for Channel Four in the UK.

A feast to befit a king and a swell gathering from the gay community, including celebrity stars, joined Tony and I with Danny La Rue officially opening Ireland's first gay B & B on 23 September 1993. It was the year that homosexuality was decriminalised in Ireland, and the press reported on our pioneering venture as *'ground-breaking, bold but a welcome venture into Irish society'*. The *Herald* reported it as a *'breath of fresh air'* whilst Nuala O'Faolain of the *Irish Times* wrote *'Liam and Tony are living witnesses to the speed with which change has happened in Ireland. Surely no other European country has changed so fundamentally and with so little anger?'*

Later in the week we did a live broadcast interview on the 'Gerry Ryan' radio programme where he said that we had *"helped to lift Irish society out of the dark ages."* Following that interview I was a frequent guest, spanning the following six years. I also did an interview for the BBC

Northern Ireland with the late David Dunseith who said *"This wonderful achievement has been welcomed broadly… do you think you might venture into Northern Ireland and open The Horse & Carriage sister ship?"* I told him that it would be an idea to consider and hopefully one day we would. We never did.

Some weeks later I received a strange telephone call from a press reporter whom I did not know, asking me for a comment on the fact that we were about to receive an award for The Horse & Carriage. I was lost for words and simply said that I couldn't speculate on something I knew nothing about. I informed Tony of the call who said to ignore it as he suspected someone was trying to pull a fast one for a cheap story. Shortly afterwards a call came through from the Dublin Chamber of Commerce to suggest that we should attend an AWARDS CEREMONY at Jury's hotel as we were in the running for an award! We were flabbergasted but overjoyed.

The day arrived and we went to Jury's as expected for the awards lunch and ceremony. As the proceedings got underway, the then Lord Mayor of Dublin, Tomas Mac Giolla, announced the nominations, "…and the winners are The Horse & Carriage Business Face Award 1993." We proudly accepted the award as Senator David Norris looked on with pride.

The Horse & Carriage was soon to prove to be very popular and successful with visiting guests from all over the world including patrons from all over Ireland, north and south. Eurovision night was one of the big spectacular party nights of the year when we would hold *Eurovision Party Night* and one year when Ireland was hosting the competition we had broadcasters from Germany and France staying, with the Germans tipped to win! They lost, and our visitors were none too happy; so much so that they left for Germany the next morning instead of the following Tuesday as planned.

In 1996, we were asked if we would be interested in putting a float into the St. Patrick's Day parade in Dublin saying that we would be the first gay entrant in the event. I said if we were going to do it we would hire a horse and carriage if it was permitted. It was, but Tony was extremely shy, and Danny La Rue jumped at the idea and through a friend he brought with him British Midland Airways as sponsors.

My uncle Frank from *ARTSCAN* did the gold-leaf design of *'The Horse & Carriage'* for either side of the carriage doors with British Midland Airways providing their advertisement board for the back of the carrier.

Four days prior to the parade, 13th March 1996, Danny La Rue was to give a *live* interview from the UK to the ever popular 'Gerry Ryan Show' here in Ireland, speaking about our participation in the parade. All checks were made and the live interview was scheduled for after 10.30am, with a patient Danny La Rue standing by. Just minutes to go, and my phone rang with the Producer of the Ryan Show telling me that the interview was postponed due to a tragedy in the UK. The interview would be recorded in the afternoon for transmission the following day, and the producer told me that Gerry Ryan would telephone me later in the day. The tragedy turned out to be *The Dunblane School Massacre* in Scotland, when a man Thomas Hamilton shot dead 16 children and one teacher before killing himself. I remember Danny being physically sick when he heard the news and spoke about the massacre in the recorded interview later that day. Gerry did phone me that evening and was pleased with the recording which was broadcasted the following morning. However the Dunblane massacre was forever etched on our minds.

The big day arrived, with Tony and I wakening at 5am to fog covering the capital city; apprehension was setting in regarding Danny's flight from London's Heathrow Airport and we were at our wits' end being so powerless. Danny phoned to say that it was highly unlikely that British Midland Airways or any other airline would be given permission to take off. I told him to remain positive, as we would have to make a decision within three hours. Tony knew that I was under extreme pressure and said that if the worst came to the worst, he would have no choice but to join me in the parade. The telephone calls between London and Dublin were frantic! It looked like Danny La Rue would not make it to Dublin.

I was about to put plan 'B' into operation when the phone rang yet again to the delightful words "We're on our way!" Our friend Michael had arrived who was acting as chauffeur for the day and a member of our staff was dispatched to ensure that the horse and carriage left on time from outside the Shelbourne Hotel. Michael, Tony and I left immediately driving through all the security barriers, with special passes, and out to Dublin Airport.

A buoyant Danny came through 'Arrivals' to applause from people waiting on passengers and straight out into the Mercedes. The show was on and we wasted no time getting back into the city centre for the parade. Tony was relieved that he didn't have to face the hordes of people lining the streets of Dublin for the national parade.

When we eventually caught up with the horse-drawn carriage, the crowds gave Danny a tumultuous warm welcome and finally the festivities had begun! We were riding into the history books as the first gay entrant in the national St. Patrick's Day Parade of 1996. Some in the VIP stand stood up and applauded, others cheered as we waved back and Danny was enjoying every second of it. He never left anyone out, waving to the crowds on both sides of the streets as the carriage moved slowly through the enthralled crowds. As we swung around into Westmoreland Street opposite Trinity College there were people hanging out of windows singing Danny's hit record 'On Mother Kelly's Doorstep'. As we were approaching O'Connell Street we were stopped on O'Connell Bridge and interviewed by RTE *(Irish Radio and Television)*. Danny reminisced about being from Cork and his ties with Ireland, and when we proceeded up O'Connell Street we were followed by a Japanese television crew and I whispered to Danny to be careful what he was saying as the microphones were live. He shouted at them, "One hung low, darlings!" I gave up and we roared laughing! We passed the GPO where Danny gave a salute in memory to the leaders 1916 Rising.

We disembarked the horse and carriage in Parnell Square and walked back to the Parnell Mooney Pub to meet up with Tony and Michael. The visit was impromptu and we stayed for an hour, with Danny delighting the crowd by singing on request his old song 'On Mother Kelly's Doorstep'.

On the road again and this time it was across the city by invitation to Baggot Street and the pub of the legendary Jack Charlton. It was my first time to meet the great man himself and he didn't disappoint; very friendly, really chatty, extremely generous with a fine spread of food and drinks galore. He reminisced about the World Cup and his memorable long career as an English footballer and Ireland manager. We could see that he loved Ireland and the following Friday, Danny was being interviewed on British Television by Alan Titchmarsh, where he thanked Tony and I, and of Jack Charlton he said, "he is considered a Saint in Ireland!"

It was time to leave the Baggot Inn after a wonderful experience and back to our apartment for some rest. Two hours later it was time to go downstairs to The Horse & Carriage with house guests, members of the gay community and family to party. Carol our housekeeper had a beautiful spread of food with drinks and the place was decorated in typical Irish tradition for St. Patrick's Day. The cooperation and coordination of our entire team was beyond reproach and we were very proud of them. After a long, hectic but most enjoyable day, it was time to leave for Killiney where we were staying the night. Michael stopped off at his parents' house where we were invited in for late night roast beef dinner which was delicious and then it was off to our final destination The Killiney Court Hotel. Mission accomplished!

After the successful opening of The Horse & Carriage, Alan Amsby expressed his desire to come back into business with us but we jointly declined his offer. When we refused the investment, his demeanour changed almost instantly and he went into a café business with others which lasted only a short period of time. On the opening night of his new venture, Tony and I did not receive an invitation and one observer referred to it as a "kick in the teeth!" We always obliged him by doing anything he requested but we hadn't realised that this was a conditional clause pertaining to our two decades of friendship! In his book *Mr Pussy: Before I Forget to Remember*, the indelible part of our mutual lives in business and friendship with all of our families spanning in excess of two decades was omitted! We realised the word 'misleading' in his alter ego image as Ireland's Misleading Lady was apt. In fairness, when Tony died he attended the funeral and so a sad part of our history had come to an end. However I will treasure the golden memories forever!

NINE

End of an Era.
Drugs, Drink & Dead Men Walking!

People who know me, will be acutely aware of the fact that I detest drugs. However, I am no saint! When I was younger I once smoked hash which put me asleep and afterwards I was vomiting for hours. I tried acid which left me paralysed for a day. One night I was judging a Halloween fancy dress competition with some celebrities and they suggested that I try cocaine, which I did, but it had no reaction until the following afternoon at a meeting; I collapsed. On another occasion my drink was spiked in a pub and I had to be rushed to hospital. That was the end of my brief history with drugs, albeit a most dreadful experience!

Back then cocaine was a very expensive drug taken by those who could afford it. Today, unfortunately, it is a very fashionable drug that can cause a multitude of problems. Some celebrities and household names were very partial to the drug. Drugs of any description were widely available in Dublin city for colossal prices, unlike today where it is more like supermarket stock!

In 1996 we were seeking an extra member of staff, and interviews were conducted accordingly and we decided to employ an Englishman to fill the vacancy. He appeared to have all the qualities we were looking for and so he was given the job. Another new member of staff asked my mother for advice upon taking up his job and she replied, "See no evil, hear no evil and speak no evil. Do the job that is expected of you and you will be fine."

We had a policy of not opening on Christmas Day as it was spent with my mother, my sister and her husband Derek, with their three children and Tony's father, Jim, at the home of Denise and Derek. It was also not our policy to accept guests at The Horse & Carriage. However, on that particular night a guest had booked in for a few days which covered Christmas Day and when we agreed that we had no option but to let him stay, we explained the situation and there was no problem on either side. Tony said that the Englishman had offered to stay as 'caretaker' as he had no other plans!

We went on to celebrate Christmas as arranged and as our house in Bridgewater Quay was let out, we were staying in our apartment and when we dropped my mum and Jim back to their respective homes we went home ourselves. As we approached The Horse & Carriage we noticed the main door ajar and when we entered there were blood-stained marks in the entrance, reception and stair handle. The guest was staying in 'Room 9' and when we went to check, he emerged with a bloodied nose and claimed he had slipped whilst out walking. The Englishman was asleep and so we cleaned up the mess and went to our apartment. When we entered we noticed on the security monitors a man standing at the top of Bow Lane East/Digges Lane opposite *INCOGNITO*. He stood there for at least forty-five minutes, smoking cigarettes in the most eerie manner. Tony wanted to go out but I pleaded with him not to go, and when the stranger left we sat for several hours watching movies with another eye on the security monitors. The next morning we checked on the guest only to find his room vacant, he had vanished and the mystery was never resolved.

We had acquired our home back in 1997, but our relationship was becoming extremely strained with both of us taking alternative days and weekends off. Our home was becoming a magnet for toxic individuals aligned to associates of Tony. The home we had worked so hard for was being seriously abused and this led to frictions within our relationship. Drink became prevalent between us and I noticed the use of drugs was beginning to raise its ugly head! A serious incident occurred in which I was advised to call in the Gardaí but I decided otherwise and demanded that the house in Bridgewater Quay be sold and the sale went through reluctantly, a mistake I regret to this day. It was with a combination of stress, anxiety, misdirection and depression that Tony attempted suicide but was caught in time by my late brother-in-law Derek. After a brief period in hospital he returned in a feeble but stable condition.

The relationship was hitting rock bottom and we agreed to see a relationship counsellor, and when the fruitless but expensive sessions were over we went on holiday to Morocco. It was a fabulous relaxing holiday and reminded me of our first holiday to Benidorm in 1978. However on the 1st March 1998, Tony's father Jim passed away. Tony felt isolated and very insecure. I tried with all my might to keep him inclusive of everything. As 1998 rolled on, we went on holiday to Chicago in the USA and this regrettably was our last holiday together. My sister Yvonne, my brother-in-law Naren and their three children flew in from South Africa for Christmas 1998, and this was the last family festive season that we celebrated.

1999 brought an avalanche of disagreements and we became like ships in the night! The drunken toxic rows fuelled with other substances were taking their toll and by summertime he told me that he had met someone else and he was leaving me. When I enquired who it was, he replied that it was the Englishman! I thought I had been hit by a bus! He said he was moving to Spain to open a pub. I was reeling in shock, not by his intention to open a pub but the fact that this obscure little 'Mr Innocent' to whom I had given a job was running away with my partner. I know it takes two to tango but that is the way I felt at the time. A close friend said, "You're better off without him," but I couldn't fathom life without him. I felt physically sick. "God doesn't exist," he once said to me and now I was beginning to wonder if he was right!

The traumatic events curled on and a mutual legal contract of separation was drawn up, no different from a divorce settlement, and he left for the Costa del Sol. I carried on running the business and attempting to remain sane but in reality I was having a mental breakdown! My beloved mother was shocked beyond belief and my entire family were devastated.

The news began to filter through to the media and I was scheduled to do a ten-minute interview on the Gerry Ryan Show which turned out to last twenty minutes. In that interview I praised Tony to the hilt and Gerry offered his deep regret saying that 25 years was a lifetime! I quoted Tony's father who used to say *"Death comes to all of us like a thief in the night"* and I said, *"Separation or divorce is like a death, it comes like a thief in the night!"* In an interview with Stephen Robinson of *Hot Press Magazine* entitled 'Gay Popular & Profitable' he wrote: *"Earlier this year the gay community was shocked and saddened by the announcement by*

Liam Ledwidge that his 25-year relationship with business partner and lover Tony Keogan had ended … I can't leave without raising the issue of the break-up of Liam's relationship with Tony Keogan. A fixture on the scene for a quarter of a century. It is difficult to imagine one without the other."

Tony, the Englishman and their cronies left for Spain to make preparations for the newly acquired bar, and within a couple of weeks he called me to say that he missed me. My heart began to flutter and I suggested we should meet on neutral territory in London; he agreed. I travelled to London City Airport and Tony flew into Heathrow and we spent the weekend together discussing the past, present and future. He said that he would be back in Dublin the following weekend but he came back with a different attitude and said that he would be returning to Spain within six weeks.

We heard that Tony and his new boyfriend were constantly arguing and that he appeared to be extremely unhappy. I was expecting the worst kind of scenario but he had made his mind up and now the legal eagles were executing the 'divorce' papers which cost both of us thousands of pounds each. Then the vilest of incidents occurred when my mother began receiving threatening telephone calls at 3 and 4 in the morning. So much so that she was petrified as she lived alone. I called one of the most senior chief superintendents of the police force who arranged senior detectives from Pearse Street Garda Station to investigate the matter.

They arranged for my mother to be interviewed at The Horse & Carriage with my sister Denise and myself. They were thorough gentlemen and covered every aspect of the criminal calls. The Gardaí assured my mother that no matter how long it took, they would find the culprit or culprits. My mother signed forms allowing the Gardaí to tap her telephone and then they paid a visit to Tony's home, in Rialto, which was left to him by his late father. They came straight back down to me and brought me up to date on their investigations and said there were other people they wanted to interview and arranged for them to be present in Tony's house the following night, and if they failed to attend a warrant would be issued for their arrest. The detectives once again came back to me and said it was highly unlikely that my mother would ever receive another threatening telephone call and that I would never hear from the alleged suspects again. We never did. It was a job well done and a couple of years later Tony recalled the incident as "Horrific and Scary" and although he was not involved, the calls came from his landline. He could never look my mother in the eye again and that is where the liaison and friendship sadly finished.

When Tony and Company decamped to Spain, it wasn't long before visitors to the pub were coming back with all kinds of horrific stories. One friend who has two holiday homes in the area came back and said the pub was open all night till dawn and customers were helping themselves, and it wasn't long before Tony returned to Dublin having lost a fortune. By 2001, I had decided to move to South Africa as by this stage I was exhausted, fed up and still very depressed over the loss of our relationship. During that year I had made several trips to scout for properties and locations in Cape Town and so I decided to make the initial move on the 8th October 2001, the eve of my 50th birthday.

Tony gave me my birthday card and present and continued to send me Christmas and birthday cards for the rest of his life. Although we were separated, we were very much in love, he often referred to our relationship as a Burton/Taylor romance! On the night of the 7th October 2001, at the top of Grafton Street, in the pelting rain and in an emotional outburst, he pleaded with me not to go to South Africa, but it was too late. I promised him a trip out to Cape Town when I got settled, and if we both felt the same way we would take it from there. We weren't to see each other for nearly four and a half years later, under tragic circumstances. I said to him as we parted that 'God did exist' and I will never forget his answer when he said, "If you say he exists, baby, then it must be true. I believe you."

My beloved late mother, Josephine Lambe Ledwidge.

My Parents' wedding day, with my Godmother, Aunt Evelyn

Me with my
grandparents Ledwidge.
1952

My grandfather Sgt Lambe – who went in
search of the psychotic De La Salle brother.

My dear grandmother Lambe and me.

My grandmother, mam, aunts and uncles
who supported me when I came out.

AMALGAMATED
ARTISTS LIMITED
18 KILDARE ST., DUBLIN
Phone : 61869

The late Frank J Bailey
Amalgamated Artists

Me in the 1970s getting ready for the road ahead.

Tony and me.

Tony, Alan and me.

**TONY AND LIAM
STUDIO ONE**
37 North Gt. Georges St.
(Around the corner from Parnell St.)

SPECIAL
Friday and Saturday Only
Dancing 11pm. - 2am.
EXCLUSIVE
Irelands gayest Night Club

**A CHOICE OF FREE
TOP QUALITY BOTTLED
WINE PER PERSON**
Or option of supper.

**OVER 21's - WITH NEAT DRESS
ESSENTIAL . ADMISSION £2**

Extra dancing nights :
Monday Wednesday and Sunday
Over 18's. Admission £1 (Members 75p)

Ireland's 1st gay commercial night club
5 December 1975

49 PARNELL SQUARE,
DUBLIN 1.

We merge with Alan Amsby AKA Mr Pussy

**Me with our German Shepherd ALK
(Amsby, Ledwidge, Keogan)**

Tony, Mam, and me in happier times.

Incognito poster

My late mother, whose advice to gay people was second to none.

Mam loved children.

**Mam at 60 at our home,
The Nora Elizabeth Suite.**

**Mum arriving for her surprise party
with Alan Amsby in the background
videotaping the occasion.**

Mum in our city apartment.

Mum in 1985, with her late sister Aileen,
friend Harry, Alan Amsby.

Alan Amsby congratulating Mum with Tony and I.

My lifelong neighbour and friend
the late Yvonne Kelly Gibbons (right),
with her partner Ann O'Connor

TEN

Flight into Conspiratorial Waters – South Africa

A mother's love is the most treasured possession we receive at birth and I will always be eternally grateful for the sustained love my mother gave to me all through her lifetime. The trusting bond we both cherished was immeasurable. On 8th October 2001, the eve of my 50th birthday, I set out for Dublin Airport accompanied by my mother and our friend Maureen to catch a flight to London on my way to Durban, South Africa.

When I got to London, I telephoned Danny La Rue, who told me to have a glass of champagne after midnight on him to celebrate my 50th! I was never a fan of champagne and I have always believed that it is highly overrated. I boarded the aircraft at London's Heathrow Airport for the eleven-hour journey to Johannesburg, with a connecting flight to Durban, my fifteenth trip to the southern tip of the African continent. It was, unbeknownst to me, to be a flight into cruel deceit, manipulation of conspiracy and corruption with devastating consequences.

As we were approaching Durban, I looked out the window as the aircraft circled and tilted over the blue seas of the Indian Ocean as it glided like a bird into Durban International Airport on a glorious summer's day on the 9th October 2001, the day of my 50th birthday. I was unaware that there were human sharks lurking below!

There were celebrations galore with my family, friends and members of the Mansoor clan who were friends of my South African family. I had known the Mansoors through family connections for a couple of years. Sadek Mansoor had recently had a boating accident and was now quadriplegic. He was a very handsome but powerful man with connections to government ministers, police chiefs and the Chief of Police himself, Jackie Selebi. I felt in safe hands.

He enquired about my intended financial investment in the country. I didn't realise that he was playing on my tired vulnerability after a long flight to gain information for his conniving plan.

Apart from resting the following day, I also knuckled down to business in preparation for my new venture in Cape Town, *Casa Blanc*. I was assisted by a top real estate agency in Durban who had gained the services of a *trusted lieutenant* Habib Khan of that organisation. It was his duty to make the preparatory plans and negotiations in relation to the purchase of the property in Melkbosstrand, Cape Town, for presentation to the solicitors and accountants. He sought and was given money for administration and work expenses, paving the way for me to meet the owner once again to do an in-depth survey of the property. After several meetings he insisted that I apply for citizenship as it would be much easier for me to deal with banks, institutions etc. I explained to Mr Khan that in practical terms, I didn't need his help in acquiring citizenship, as my brother-in-law and members of my family were South African and I could use them as reference. "But I go to the department on Umgeni Road every day, it's like a second home to me so I will be able to process this application very quickly!" It seemed practical and reasonable that he should pursue the application in light of his experience and his frequent visits to the department to deal with such applications, it was better for him to do it in order to save time. I conceded and regrettably allowed him to pursue the application. He required money for 'lodgement processing fees', accountants, solicitors and administration fees which he was given. A total of R47,000 (£4,700 in those days). He also required medical, police and tax clearance from Ireland which I had brought with me. He also took my fingerprints and said the whole process could take two weeks or less.

I flew with my PA for ten days to Cape Town for a week to commence negotiations. The owner of the property, a very affable lady, was extremely cooperative and welcoming and I knew that we were singing from the same hymn sheet. Tony always showed concern and telephoned me from time to time. I knew by his mood after a high-profiled separation, he was finding it difficult to let go of the strings, even though he had publicly said we were finished! The flame was still glimmering between us.

However, after the trip to Cape Town I returned to Durban, where the Mansoors were more than anxious to enquire about the developments to date. I noticed that Habib Khan was slacking after receiving a lot of money and he wasn't answering his phone. I was concerned! He eventually made contact by arriving at my family home, all apologies, with what seemed to be very legitimate excuses and he said that he needed my passport for two hours to bring it to the Department of Home Affairs. When I enquired what this was for, he said that he needed to get it stamped with an extension of my visa as it would be necessary to proceed with the mortgage application. I thought it more prudent for me to accompany him to the department as I was the holder of the passport, but he passed it off stridently saying there was no need as it was only a matter of a stamp. He said the application was successful and that I would receive temporary citizenship until the matter was finalised which was only a matter of time. I hesitantly agreed.

Whilst he was away I discussed it with my family who were furious that he had taken my passport. He arrived back in the early hours of the afternoon, beaming with joy, along with my passport stamped 'married with spouse' and a marriage certificate! My heart stopped! I was aghast with fury. What was the purpose of this? He said it was to substantiate my application for citizenship! He had me married to a Tamil widow, mother of four grown-up daughters, named Muniaama Moodley, in the black township of Lamontville. The marriage was supposed to have taken place in the black township of Lamontville on 31 October 2001. So here I was, a well-known openly gay man married to a black woman from a black township, a place I've never heard of or seen in my life. It was bordering on absurdity. It was an action totally unheard of and to me it was mere tripe! An argument ensued and he left and the real estate agency refused to accept responsibility. However, hot on his heels were the Mansoors. Sadek Mansoor went to work immediately by telephoning his alleged friend, the Minister of Home Affairs, Mangosuthu Buthelezi, or so I was led to believe. It was also alleged that Jackie Selebi, Chief of Police in South Africa and a friend of the Mansoors, was to be brought in to deal with Khan. Selebi was later to fall from grace and was brought to justice over corruption charges highlighted by an Irishman Paul O'Sullivan from Cork who spent years on the case. This was a significant fall as Jackie Selebi was held in high esteem by international police forces.

What transpired in the intervening week and following a lot of discussion it was decided to allow Sadek Mansoor's brother-in-law, Ahmed Jacob Mansoor, to assist me in the sale negotiation of the property to pursue a good deal. Ahmed Mansoor, a property developer, businessman and entrepreneur was under the direction of Sadek Mansoor. Habib Khan had faded from the scene altogether and I was assured that my passport would be rectified. I was warned not to go near the police or the Irish authorities as his friend Mangosuthu Buthelezi, Minister for Foreign Affairs and Jackie Selebi would deal with the matter.

Meanwhile, summer in South Africa is extremely hot and I was commuting between Durban and Cape Town with my business plan. It was decided to move full time to Cape Town on the 26th December 2001, with the expectation of moving into *Casa Blanc* in the first week in January 2002.

My PA and I took to the road in a Condor as planned for the two-day driving trip to Cape Town to meet up with the Capetonians team. The scenic route to the mother city is truly remarkable and the majestic skyline of the mother city was now in sight, surrounded by the intriguing Table Mountain. We booked into our hotel and the air conditioning was a blessed relief from the midday sun.

Once again I was to experience delays as we entered the New Year, but the most explosive of them all was when I discovered R600,000 (£60,000 in those days) had been transferred from my bank account into that of the Mansoor account. I fell backwards into the chair with fright. I was numb beyond all imagination. I immediately called to meet them as a matter of the gravest urgency and they asked, "Are you in Durban?" I informed them that I was in Cape Town but that I was getting the next available flight, but they said they could only meet with me on Monday night 14th January. I left straight away from Cape Town to Durban, staying at my family home. I could feel the tides of confusion wrestling with my angry emotions. I could not comprehend the deceit.

On Monday I booked into the Holiday Inn nearby where Sadek Mansoor lived and where he conducted business. I waited patiently, and at 7pm precisely I arrived at his apartment, overlooking the sea front, only to find the Mansoor brothers there in force. An AK47 sat nearby, which was not unusual as he carried the weapon around with him when he was an able-bodied person but it was a stark reminder of his power. When I questioned him about the transfer of money he reminded me that I had attended the bank before Christmas with Ahmed and transferred the money. I remembered that I had attended the bank as suggested and the individual in the bank was a relative of his, with whom Ahmed had a private 15 minutes' meeting before I entered. I said I had transferred money for the Condor and flights to another airline company where another relative of his worked and paid for flights for my mother and Maureen who were arriving on St. Patrick's Day. As it transpired, I had paid twice the amount for the flights and Ahmed Mansoor said it was his commission. I was furious. He produced another document which stated that I had given him 'Power of Attorney' to deal with the owner of

Casa Blanc but my argument was that this did not constitute power over my personal finances of which he had no legitimate control.

He told me not to be worrying as I was half way there to purchasing *Casa Blanc* and the papers would be ready in two weeks for signing in Cape Town. Ahmed would travel down to represent him and that I would be in residence in February. He handed me R1000 that he had managed to retrieve from Habib Khan! He showed me documents to prove his point. The pressure was beginning to lift and I thought I felt that there was a glimmer of hope and I left under restrained circumstances.

I took the lift to the bottom of the block and walked back to my hotel and, as I was walking on this very hot night, I noticed five or six Indian thugs approaching. Within a flash I felt a blow to my face as my glasses flew into oblivion; they kicked me in the groin, ribs, stomach back and head. I was crouched on the ground with blood streaming down my face from my nose and elsewhere. A concerned passing motorist jumped out of his car and intervened, otherwise I would have died from my injuries. He helped me to my feet and then vanished. I had been robbed of my cell phone, my wallet containing R2000, my gold watch, a gold necklace bought for me by Yvonne and Naren for my 40th birthday and a file containing important files relating to *Casa Blanc*. I staggered, bloodied, and in extreme pain back to the hotel without anyone helping me. I managed to get up to my room on the sixteenth floor and had to request a member of the staff to let me in. I telephoned my sister and Sadek Mansoor from my room. I was amazed at the expediency of Mansoor, as to how he managed to get to me so quickly in a wheelchair and with his aide followed by six police officers. He pretended to be shocked but in hindsight he was shocked that I wasn't finished off! He ordered brandy for everyone including the police and when I eventually left the hotel I was handed the bill for the drinks. My brother-in-law wanted me to go to hospital but I refused and Mansoor arranged for a police officer to stand guard outside the door all night.

I was aching all over and my left eye was closed up, but my brother-in-law returned the following morning with medication. Meanwhile in the middle of the night my telephone rang and when I answered a strange voice threatened me to leave the country immediately or face the consequences! He told me to walk over to the window and open the curtain and look out at the sea and said, "Look at the calm sea, its inhabitants the great sharks are waiting for you. You have one week to get out! Go back to your homeland." The phone went dead, I was petrified. I called in the police officer who took a report and I called my assistant and we gathered my belongings, and in an extremely feeble state we left for the airport and took the next available flight to Cape Town.

I went straight to my hotel and collapsed and woke up in the former Christian Bernard Hospital where I stayed for five days. I had to be released for a few hours to go to an optician to get new glasses as my former set had been misplaced during the mugging. However, on the third day Ahmed Jacob Mansoor arrived and ordered me out of bed to meet with the solicitors, and in a bold move he insisted on seeing the solicitor of the vendor. A row occurred between them and Mansoor stayed overnight to continue the next day. He was a bully and a nasty individual who treated women like pieces of dirt. I was sick, exhausted and worried over the telephone call to which Mansoor stated, *"Those are the henchmen of that dragon here in Cape Town, don't worry about it."* Nothing could be further from the truth!

We eventually moved in to Casa Blanc on a month-by-month rental basis until an agreed mortgage settlement had been reached. The banks had agreed in principle to lend the mortgage. Although I was still not totally fit, one of my first engagements was to invite everyone from the tourist industry to *Casa Blanc* as I was interested not only in promoting it around South Africa but a holiday destination for Irish people to come to. Plans were afloat to arrange a flight to Dublin with South Africans to explore Ireland and the same flight would return with Irish people wishing to explore South Africa. It was my intention to meet with gay groups and do something similar.

St. Patrick's Day arrived and my mother and Maureen arrived for a six weeks' visit. They stayed at *Casa Blanc* and I brought them to see the sights of the Mother City including Table Mountain.

However, towards the end of the third week, rows between the Mansoors and the vendor's solicitor erupted once again and I was informed by the banks that the mortgage application had been refused. When I asked for my deposit back they said there was no deposit as Mansoor held the security deposit! It was time to leave and thrash the matter out with the Mansoors in Durban as the owner of *Casa Blanc* had been subjected to hassle and grievances way beyond her limits by Mansoor. My mother and Maureen flew up to Durban to our family home and my PA and I drove the two-day journey back, going from the frying pan into the fire!

ELEVEN

Arrest and Detention

On April 23rd 2002, the sun was beating down fiercely on this humid day in the southern hemisphere city of Durban, South Africa. My dear late friend Maureen, who was in her late seventies, sat pensively in the shade, avidly reading one of her latest favourite novels. My mother, now one month from her seventieth birthday, was showering in preparation for a sad farewell to a dear friend "Nana", who had died at the weekend in Phoenix. My niece studied and listened to music with not a care in the world. Our loveable family dog Cuddles was curled up in the lounge in ignorant bliss, as Clementine, our housekeeper went about her daily chores. I had written out the sympathy cards and was attaching them to the wreaths, their aromatic bouquets enhanced by the sun that shone majestically through the open window.

At precisely 10.45am, a car pulled up outside the security gates. Clementine recognised the vehicle as one from the Department of Home Affairs. The barking from Cuddles startled the two men as they waited to gain entry. Maureen's curiosity tempted her to abandon her novel as she walked towards the reception lounge, enquiring about the loud commotion that surrounded her. They had produced their ID and announced themselves as Alpheus Sibila and Colin Bigela, officers from the department of Home Affairs representing Minister Mangosuthu Buthelezi.

The nightmare was on the verge of beginning. I was about to descend into a pit with its fire of brimstone, whilst the Mansoors, our former friends and conspirators, danced merrily with the devil in an elaborate scam so carefully orchestrated that I stood no chance of fighting alone with crooked officials from a foreign Government. I have since wondered in hindsight, if Nelson Mandela's dreams and ideals of a new South Africa, or his incarceration of twenty-seven years were all in vain.

I greeted both gentlemen and offered them tea or a cold drink, but they declined. They asked to see my documentation, passport and my visa, saying they were acting on an enquiry of complaint, but they refused to reveal their source.

"The Mansoors no doubt," I exclaimed.

A flood of perspiration erupted from the forehead of Alpheus Sibila as he dropped some papers to the floor and attempted to compose himself.

"I am not at liberty to say," he said.

Colin Bigela held his hand on his gun, which was clenched into his holster at the hip, his eyes wandered everywhere, attempting to avoid my defiant gaze.

I produced my passport and they enquired about my visa.

"This married with spouse. What is this? Where is your wife?" they protested, knowing in their hearts and souls that there was no wife.

"You have an extension to your visa and you have a South African wife. Where is she?" demanded a perspiring Sibila.

I explained that I was purchasing a property in Cape Town and had engaged the services of an Estate Agent who sent us their representative, a Mr Habib Khan, who had deceived us by producing this marriage certificate. I explained that our friends, the ever influential Mansoors, allegedly friends with Minister Buthelezi, had taken over and had taken full responsibility to have the matter rectified. Sibila became agitated whilst Bigela retained a tight grip on his gun.

"I think we should go," said Colin Bigela, dismissing my argument.

"Go where?" I asked.

"To the Department of Home Affairs on Umgeni Road," said Sibila.

I told them that it was imperative that they speak to my brother-in-law at his surgery, who would explain that we didn't need false marriages or the Khans of this world to vouch for me in my quest for citizenship, as my family were South African. I immediately rang Naren and when he heard of the impending crisis, he demanded to speak with them and told them that we were going to a funeral and that the pending matter would have to wait until the following day.

Sibila was frustrated and embarrassed and said that he would need to call his boss. He sought permission to use the landline, but having spoken to him, we were told the reply was one of regret stating, "Which is more important, the funeral or the documentation? The dead are gone, they have no worries and you must come now."

The voice on the other end of the phone was a man called Terence Menthe. Maureen intervened but they reassured her that I would be back for the funeral.

"Have you no respect for the dead, young man?"

"We are only acting upon orders," replied Bigela.

"Whose orders?" she demanded.

"The Minister has to get to the bottom of this," he retorted.

"Are the Mansoors up to something?" she enquired.

He blushed again.

"I will make sure he is back for the funeral," he said rather dismissively, wishing to exit the house as quickly as possible.

"Will you drive him back for the funeral?" she asked.

"He will be back for that, I promise," said a perspiring Bigela as Maureen kissed me affectionately with an anxious look on her aging face.

I left Mobeni Heights on Tuesday 23 April, 2002, and was not back until Tuesday 09 July. This was a brutal, tortuous period of eleven weeks, 77 days, and an astounding, but disturbing story that was blazoned across the media on two nations which would have everlasting effects.

On arrival at the department on Umgeni Road in Grayville, Durban, I was greeted with faces of hostility from a group of officials in a large open glass windowed room. A white man in his late forties, whom I later discovered was Terence Menthe, was present and who himself was on the verge of arrest in connection with the perpetration of the bogus marriage in collaboration with Habib Khan. Khan was never caught. However, a trembling Menthe told me to write a statement as to where and from whom I obtained the extended visa and marriage certificate. My mobile phone was constantly ringing, with family and friends seeking information on what was going on. I was only able to relay events as they emerged in front of me.

There was an air of conspiracy and I distrusted everyone. A top official poked his nose eerily into my face and asked me several times whom I knew in the department who had issued these false documents. I repeatedly informed him that I knew of no official or contact, but when he tired of ranting and raving, his colleague continued in a threatening tone and warned me that I would never leave South Africa until the traitors and collaborators were caught. I asked for a glass of water, but was refused.

My head was pounding and my clothes were sticking to my skin in the intense heat. Terence Menthe produced a large photograph of Habib Khan and asked, "Is this the individual who gave you the marriage certificate?" I replied it was and he then asked me his name. When I mentioned his name, another official screamed, "The fucker is like Houdini, we can never catch him. First the Australians, then the Chinese and now the fucking Irish. Someone in this department is helping him with these marriage certificates and visas," he fumed to his amused colleagues. Menthe blushed profusely and was trembling as he picked up my statement.

"So you know the Mansoors?" he asked, turning ashen-faced and shaking.

I began to watch him carefully and my perception of him proved to be accurate. Two weeks later, he was arrested on suspicion of fraud and corruption in connection with my case, held in custody and dismissed from his job. In order for Menthe and Khan to make money out of me, they conspired to produce a false marriage certificate to maximise my stay in the Republic of South Africa. The ironic thing about this whole affair is that I never knew Menthe or any of his colleagues but we eventually heard that he stubbornly refused to cooperate with the Mansoors and that this was his ultimate downfall.

I was then attacked abusively by a top official and another who seemed to be second in command. They screamed as they fired books at me in frustration, "Who is this wife of yours?"

As I attempted to answer, they continued, "Where did you get this fucking certificate from?"

Once again, I was denied the opportunity to answer. Then came the glass of water but instead of them giving it to me to drink they threw it in my face.

"Are you in the IRA?"

I did not reply. There was silence.

"Well are you?" they asked.

I looked at them straight in the eye and refused to answer such an atrocious question. They looked baffled, searching fruitlessly for answers and trying to formulate a framework as they went on.

The department of Home Affairs was riddled with corruption and there was daily headline news regarding fake marriages. Someone, somewhere, was making a lot of money out of it. One thing was evident and that was the fear they had of the Mansoors. They left the room without saying a word.

Within minutes they returned and looked at me spitefully and said, "We heard you are a member of the IRA. Now, either you are going to confess to this, or we are going to get a statement out of you one way or the other. Now it's up to you."

"Prove it, prove it!" I screamed in anger. "Have a look at my Police clearance from Ireland. This proves that I have never been in trouble, so what the hell are you trying to do, get a nice confession so that you will be patted on the back and rewarded? Anyway what would I expect from you lot when you think the Republic of Ireland is in the UK?"

They looked shocked as I stood in front of them and after a silent pause one said, "Not bad for a queer boy."

They were bullying me with a groundless argument in an attempt to coerce me into giving them a false statement.

Another government agent entered and came close to my ear and whispered, "Has that fucker Buthelezi got anything to do with this?"

He smirked.

"Why don't you pick up your telephone and invite the Minister down here and we'll settle the matter like gentlemen."

He looked disturbingly into my eyes and said, "What about Selebi?"

"Who?" I replied?

"Jackie Selebi, Chief of Police."

"I know nothing about him," I replied.

"He is a friend to the Mansoors."

I remained silent. The door swung open and the two dangerous puppets Alpheus and Colin entered. They spoke in Afrikaans, after which I was summoned to accompany the pair. I thought I was being taken home, but I was wrong. I was told that I was being held at CR Swart overnight, police holding cells downtown. I was dumbfounded.

I was humiliatingly transported in broad daylight in an open jeep through the streets of Durban and onwards to a filthy den of iniquity, as the general public watched in amazement. They purposely drove down Marine Parade on the beachfront past the bars and restaurants that we used to frequent and past the residence of the Mansoors. I was their accolade on parade.

"Look what we caught. Look what we can do to the white man," was their modus operandi.

We arrived into an enclosed yard and drove through open gates to this outer office, where there was a crowd of black youths in handcuffs and shackles staring inquisitively. My mobile phone was obvious in my pocket as I tried to conceal it. I noticed their curious black faces, speechless in movement staring at me with their eyes following my every move. One black young man, who was wandering suspiciously around without handcuffs, suddenly grabbed my phone and dialled a number and began to speak, before a guard grabbed it from his hand and whipped him around the head with a belt. I was horrified.

"He was only ringing Harare, probably trying to get his mammy to get him out of here! He should have thought of the consequences before he crossed the border," the guard said to me sarcastically as he handed the phone back. Harare is the capital of Zimbabwe where the despot Mugabe ruled at that time.

I was called into a small office to raucous laughter as one said, "It's our turn to get the fucking white man." Their choice of colloquial and foul language was extensive.

A jolly guard took my fingerprints and said, "I'll isolate you from these hungry monsters, my man, to a private cell." I was relieved.

The cells were dark and grimy, with excrement plastered across the walls, the stench was unbearable. The toilet had a small wall partition, there was no shower, washing facilities or running water. I was told to take a foam mattress and two blankets that were so lice-riddled that they almost moved by themselves.

At 4.50pm I had a visit from Shaun, who buried his father Nana earlier in the day, the funeral I should have attended. Shaun was a part-time officer with the Beach Patrol Police and was accompanied by a police captain who was a friend of his, whom I had met the previous weekend to discuss what should be done with the Mansoors. We discussed the case and the Captain was at a loss as to how they beat us to it, in view of my meeting with two of his inspectors the night before. He said he was completing a dossier on the Mansoors and was valiantly going to have them arrested on outstanding investigations. I was unaware at the time that the two genial inspectors from the night before were in fact on the side of the Mansoors and hence the swift operation.

They left and, within an hour, Shaun returned with Valpre water, cigarettes and snacks. We discussed the Captain's visit and the irony of the efficient tactics in the case. The Mansoors were involved in a multi-million rands' scandal which involved a lot of high-profiled people and at least one Government Minister. According to some police I had met they all wanted to bust them, but now at this stage who was I to believe?

Later in the evening, the kindly police captain accompanied my distraught mother to the holding cells, as Maureen was under sedation and unable to travel. As much as we were all in shock, it was particularly stressful for my mother and Maureen. There was little we could say except that my sister and brother-in-law had retained a lawyer and were working around the clock for my release, which we saw as being imminent the following day. I could see the agony in my mother's tired, sad eyes and told her to return home to rest, which she reluctantly did, crying as she left. She was never to recover from the torment.

At 9.33pm they imprisoned another young man from Zimbabwe, who cried all night long over the prospect of going to Westville Prison or being deported back to his dreaded homeland. I gave him some of my snacks, which he ate speedily out of intense hunger, but I found it difficult to communicate with him as his command of the English language was limited.

As dawn broke I was told to help in the collection of the lice-riddled mattresses and blankets and store them on top of each other in an empty cell, as all other prisoners were gathered together in one large cell. I was covered in lice, with my skin irritating to the point of spilling drops of blood from constant scratching. I was covered in filth and I could smell the foul odour from my body.

At 10am a white good-looking Afrikaner was confined in the same cell, waiting for his wife to pay 1800 rands (£1,800 in those days) for traffic fines. We began talking and he asked me what I was doing in there and when I told him briefly he was shocked. He referred to the inmates and guards in derogatory terms stating:

"You must do all in your power to get out of this sewer, they would kill you in an instant. If they take you to Westville Prison, you may as well forget about it, because they will have you for breakfast, dinner and tea. The members [*Prison wardens*] are not safe up there. They'd rape anything. Especially a white man, rape is a disease with them," he said insightfully as if speaking from experience.

I was scared, but discounted the idea of Westville Prison, since this was for criminals and gangsters and there was no way I would end up there. At exactly 2pm, the Afrikaner was released and the Zimbabwean and I were brought to the front reception. I was convinced I would be released until I saw Alpheus Sibila and Colin Bigela lurking about like two scorpions.

"We are going to Umgeni Road for processing and onwards to Westville Prison," said Bigela.

My heart stopped. I knew I did not have the stamina or the courage to face this ordeal. My whole world had crumbled around me.

Westville Prison is one of the most notorious prisons in South Africa. It houses thousands of inmates, men, women and children and is famous for the gangs of 26's (26-year-olds) who engage in stabbings, violence and torture and the 28's (28-year-olds), who are in pursuit of sex and prostitution. The gang rapes are not only a pleasurable pursuit but also a lucrative way of surviving, like the beast of the jungle. It is known for its vicious gangs of thuggery and violent attacks on inmates from murderers, drug lords, drug addicts, schizophrenics, common thugs and rapists including baby rapists. This derelict, broken institution of humanity is a breeding ground for warped and dangerous criminal minds that produces evil negativity. Dagga *(Cannabis)* is smoked all day long and although the authorities allege they were doing something about it, the answer is they were scared to do anything. The judges refused to inspect Westville Prison for fear of being kidnapped, harmed or killed.

Prisoners were out of their minds on dagga which fuelled their anger and oppression.

We were told to get into the prison wagon with ten others as we proceeded towards Umgeni Road and the Department of Home Affairs. I was severely dehydrated and the lack of oxygen and foul body odour, including my own, was sickening. When we arrived, I was once again placed under scrutiny and interrogation from eight officials, which was very intimidating and aggressive. This time they questioned me about the amount of money I had given to Habib Khan and the Mansoors and they demanded to know to whom I had given money to at the Department of Home Affairs. Once again I protested vehemently that I knew no officials, that I never paid anyone at the department and that I had no contact with any officials at the department of Home Affairs. I explained that I had simply gone to an estate agent with a view to purchasing a property in Cape Town and they in turn sent me Habib Khan to do groundwork in Durban. Khan required fees for administration, accountants and solicitors, which he received. He also required police clearance from Ireland, along with a personal letter from An Garda Siochana *(Irish Police Force)*, tax clearance and medical records including a chest X-ray. Instead of coming back with an extension to my visa, he returned with a marriage certificate stating that I had married a black Tamil widow in the black township of Lamontville.

A snap aggressive outburst came when the senior official roared at all officials to line up with their backs against the wall. He then grabbed me, pushed my face into the faces of the uneasy officials and screamed, "Is it him? Or is it her?" The circus show came to an abrupt end when my lawyer Pregasen Marimuthu entered.

He immediately questioned my detention, but was promptly informed that I was an alien living in the country. He told them that I was no threat to the state and, in view of the fact that my family lived in South Africa and were South African citizens, he saw no objectionable reason to the granting of a visa in conjunction with the Irish Embassy in South Africa. They were further reminded that I had come to their country to invest money and to create employment with a full business plan, but had been defrauded.

The lawyer suggested privately to Alpheus Sibila a possible fine in order to gain my release and he replied, "30,000 rands [£3,000 in those days]." A female official, upon hearing his reply, gasped in disbelief. Sibila walked into another room. The female official approached and said, "No such thing," but was unable to continue as Terence Menthe arrived back on the scene, looking a lot calmer than the day before. He told the lawyer it would cost 6,500 rands, a fine of 1,500 rands to the department and 5,000 rands for an airline ticket.

"He hasn't been given deportation orders," exclaimed Pregasen.

"No," said Menthe, "but he will be. In the meantime he will have to stay at Westville Prison."

"This is absurd. You cannot send a man to prison on a ridiculous trumped-up charge. This man is an upstanding citizen of Ireland, a welcome visitor to our country, an investor and pioneer in his field. He has done nothing wrong and his family are prepared to vouch for him until the matter has been resolved," said Marimuthu.

"It's out of my hands," said a smirking official who himself was on the verge of a massive and humiliating downfall.

TWELVE

Conspiracy to Incarcerate

It was the second time in one day that I squeezed into the prison van in sweltering heat, a broken, lonely man consumed by dread as to what lay ahead. Thirty years previously I had been a passenger in my aunt's car which was involved in an accident on Dublin's Naas dual carriageway, leaving me with a permanent back injury. As we made the forty-minute drive to Westville Prison, the driver constantly jammed on the breaks, throwing the ten of us forward and sending excruciating pain through my spinal cord. Sufferers of back pain will confirm that it can be quite debilitating. I had no medication and I was exhausted, which only exacerbated the pain.

As we approached the prison, the driver appeared to manoeuvre over rocky terrain and as the wagon bounced and backed up to a prison gate, we were thrown around like cattle. I sustained a large painful bruise to my back. We eventually disembarked and there to greet us was a large filthy yard with dozens of urine-soaked mattresses strewn across the ground. In the upper section of the extended overhead prison building, all manner of clothing from underwear to vests and uniforms was hanging from small barred windows. The foul odour was insufferable as we were pushed into a high-ceilinged room where our fingerprints and details were taken. I was given a card which simply read 'Alien'.

On completion we passed through a large room, and what I witnessed left me frozen. There was over one hundred men and boys lying on the floor, some spread-eagled, some resembling characters from a Vietnam movie or victims of violence, with eyes hanging, broken legs and head injuries. The sufferers of HIV/AIDS recoiled into corners like lepers, ashamed of their appearance. The guards kept shouting, "Keep going, keep going"; I stalled both in agony with back pain and shock until a guard pushed me to the floor. I lay in agony until two prisoners helped me to my feet. The guard looked at me with bulging eyes, spat in my face and said, "Keep going you fucking idiot." I stared him eyeball to eyeball and said, "God forgive you, these people are human beings not crocodiles at the end of a river." He licked his lips and replied, "Maybe you want to join the crocodiles, these are human waste and you are nobody, you are an alien." He grabbed me by my wet shirt and told me to proceed to this very large cell.

There were groups of more prisoners waiting for incarceration and one hundred and thirty of us were taken to "C" section, classified "Alien Wing" and all of us were told to join the already overcrowded cell, which increased the head count to over two hundred in a cell fit for thirty people sleeping in bunk beds. I was told that Medium "C" was the hub of corrupt activities within the prison. I later learned that corruption was endemic within the prison itself.

The few bunk beds were taken up and there were sponge mattresses on top of each other in a corner, along with lice-riddled blankets which were strewn on the floor at night. There was one rock-hard pillow. The overcrowding was so intense we had to sleep standing up against the slimy walls. It was horrendous and the smell of dagga was stifling and everywhere you looked the inmates were smoking and sharing it. I had never seen anything like it in my life.

The dreary faces and sunken eyes of some was an indication that these people were seriously ill, their vacant faces so miserable and barely alive in a human cesspit of deplorable indignation. Some had chronic vomiting and diarrhoea, using the one and only open toilet in the entire room with no privacy whatsoever. The skin on their emaciated bodies was dry and they were covered in blotches. It was heart-breaking watching them desperately trying to move their skeletal frames around the heaving room. I knew that at least half a dozen of these people were in the final stages of the AIDS' virus. I had never seen so many helpless at the one time, with no medication, no one to talk to and no one to care for them.

The inmates had come from Nigeria, Angola, Botswana, Lesotho, Malawi, Mozambique, Namibia, Zimbabwe and two from China, two from India and I was the only European in the cell.

I lit up a cigarette and immediately they were around me requesting a 'drag'. In the surrounding chaos, a voice bellowed in the background and the instant silence prevailed as the crowd around me slowly parted like the Red Sea. There in front of me stood a young man, hardened-faced man with a deep scar on his face staring piercingly through my eyes, but with a quaint smile on his face.

"Hello," he said, "I'm Scar Face and I am in charge of this beautiful suite at the Westville Hotel." We both laughed and from that moment in time he was my saving grace. Although a ruthless criminal, he was kind and generous, witty and intelligent. He was 26 years of age and had a great deal of respect for me as his elder. He commanded that cell like an army general, he introduced me to many of the inmates who told me of their predicaments that led them to South Africa. Some fled from war and oppression, hunger and starvation seeking asylum, ruthless dictators and the list went on.

I was introduced to Justin and George, and was allowed to sit amongst them. I could see that George was very sick, but we never spoke about it. He was constantly scuffling between the top corner of the cell where we sat on a filthy couch to the bottom corner next to the open toilet which catered for everyone. Justin informed me that George was very sick, but he was enjoying my company. When I politely told him that I was no great company to anyone because of the predicament I was in, he sadly informed me that George was dying and had very little time left. I felt ashamed and selfish. I asked Justin why he and others were not taken to hospital. He responded with concern, "There is no room and anyway when you are dying you are not allowed to die in the prison hospital because you are taking up another bed."

I found it absolutely extraordinary that these people were consigned to the scrap heap, with indignation and insult to their humanitarian rights, with a careless attitude from the authorities.

They were an amazing bunch of people. They had medium-sized saw blades, which they connected with an electric wire to a tin can so that they could place a pot on top with water to make tea or boil potatoes illegally in the cell.

We only had one small washbasin and one open toilet bowl for all two hundred of us and by now, I was beginning to feel the full strain of the situation. It was difficult to sleep on the hard floor with the noise and lurking danger. There was a great deal of coughing and whispering and strange devious movements in the cell which was unnerving.

The prisoners who had to go to court arose at 5am and the rest of us at 6am for a head count, followed by breakfast which consisted of cold porridge which I didn't eat and two slices of burnt toast with tea. We were fed through a half opened window like wild animals. The only other meal of the day consisted of samp, Mieliepap or minced fish which still contained fragments of bones and was more like cat food than something fit for human consumption.

On the 25th of April, my mother and Maureen came to visit me and were visibly shocked at my appearance with greasy hair and a partial beard. It was not right for a mother to see her son locked up like a wild animal, which hurt her so deeply. They were on the verge of vomiting from the foul stench in the prison. The visit took place in a large caged area where it was difficult to hear at times with prisoners screaming from beatings by the members nearby. The visit lasted five minutes with a message from by brother-in-law that I would be released by 2pm. I was relieved and started counting the minutes.

I returned to the area where Scar Face was waiting to bring me back to the cell. A winding walkway surrounded the area, which was secured by ground-to-ceiling iron bars dividing the area from the arena, which was flooded by water due to a broken pipe. It was like walking in a sewer. As we made our way back, there was a hell of a commotion as two young men in front of us who were returning from the visiting area were attacked by a youth trying to rob them of the goods they had received whilst on their visit. An officer, or a member as they are called, came charging down like Hercules and beat the living daylights out of him with a baton. His blood squirted in all directions, like a lamb being slaughtered. He fell to the winding floor, tumbling as he went, screaming horrifically as the member booted and beat him and then demanded that he clean the place up.

As time ticked by, in the early afternoon I became more tense, awaiting news of my release. Some prisoners asked me where Ireland was and if we had millions of priests and nuns! Their simplistic view of Ireland was amusing if not frightening. At 2.55pm, I gave Scar Face some money to buy a telephone card from the dealers and I called my sister Yvonne. I could tell by her voice that she was stressed. Her heart was bleeding, but her spirit was hopeful. She was waiting for a call from our lawyer, and the day was dragging on, but she tried with all her blessed might to keep me happy and assured me that everything that was feasible was being done.

At 3.05, we were locked up for the rest of the day and night and my heart sank to a new low. In the meantime, I was unaware that the department of Home Affairs had agreed to accept the 6,500 rands (£650 in those days) for my release, only to change their minds two hours later. They had given my lawyer and brother-in-law the complete run around all day and I was none the wiser. I was unaware of what had transpired on the outside and the hours seemed endless as nightfall slowly approached. At 8pm, the Chief in charge put his head through the grid and called my name. As I struggled to make my way to the steel gates through the crowded cell, I hoped that I was going to be released, but as the gate swung open I was instructed, "Stand back, stand back, prisoners entering."

Thirty extra prisoners filed passed as the Chief stepped forward and said, "You look awful, have you eaten?"

"No," I replied. "Is there any news?"

"Yes, your brother-in-law left this bag for you. He said he was late today and he will visit tomorrow. Now eat something, good night."

The gate was slammed in my face. I was devastated. I noticed George was missing from his usual corner and I asked after his whereabouts in the crowds of inmates in the one cell. At that moment there was a disturbance at the top of the room as prisoners began banging on the steel door seeking attention. Zak, a prisoner and sufferer of AIDS had died as George tried to comfort him. He had spent his last moments in this dungeon of hell, with no assistance and no last rites. It was a poignant moment as I watched this twenty-one-year-old being irreverently placed in a white coffin on its way to the mortuary. If Zak's family wanted his body, they had to collect it within twenty-four hours and pay 50 rands (£5 in those days) or his body would be cremated and forgotten about. It pained me deeply to witness such a sad end to such a young life, but he was only the first that I was to witness die on undignified ground during my stay at Westville. It was a haven of destruction, an isolated den of gross neglect and depravity. My problems paled into insignificance.

On the morning of Friday 26 April, my name was called again and when I answered a member said, "Take your belongings, you're free to go." I was filled with joy. Scar Face screamed, "Hallelujah!" I gathered my belongings and gave the remaining packets of cigarettes and money to Scar Face to share among his fellow inmates and proceeded down the long walkway to freedom, or so I thought.

The member who escorted me said, "You are going back to Ireland." I was elated as I waited for papers to be processed in that large ugly gathering room where we had been on Wednesday night. In an instant, my life flashed in front of me as I caught sight of Alpheus Sibila of Home Affairs. My dreams were shattered as the euphoria was replaced by horror. He looked at me with venomous eyes and tore my docket up, leaving the paper flittering and falling to the floor.

"We are going to Court at Chatsworth," he said sarcastically.

"For what?" I asked.

"To lodge these charges," he replied.

I was not allowed to see the charge sheet and was told abruptly to get into the prison van. I was alone in the van and as I looked through the caged windows, I knew he was off course and not heading towards Chatsworth. We were completely off track. I then noticed the sign pointing to the airport, with Colin Bigela and another, whom I did not recognise from Home Affairs, driving alongside us. It was spooky.

We pulled into the car park at Durban International Airport where they disembarked from the two vans and gathered in a group, talking privately amongst themselves. The three of them approached the wagon and looked inside at me. Two of them walked a short distance away and Colin Bigela came to the side grilled open panel and said, "Listen Liam," nervously twirling his thumps, "We don't like what is happening any more than you do, but you and your family are making it difficult for us with that fancy lawyer. Perhaps we could reach an agreement?"

"Like what?" I asked.

"The people involved are all very high-profiled individuals and Minister Buthelezi cannot afford an international scandal. We can have you back with your family today, if you agree to leave the country within a week, say for 6,000 rands [£600 in those days] and no-one will know about it."

I pretended to be polite and asked, "What about Home Affairs, your department?"

"We will cover that after you leave the country and if you change your statement against the Mansoors—"

I interrupted and once again pretended to play ball "What about my lawyer and the Irish Embassy in Pretoria?" I asked quietly, as I stared him in the face.

"Fuck the lawyer and fuck the Irish Embassy," he said in a curt rage. "Fuck you too," I replied.

"I feel sorry for you," he said and walked away. We then proceeded to Chatsworth and not to the courthouse as had been indicated, but to Bayview Police Station. The temperature was continuing to rise and I was feeling extremely weak. We stood outside the two wagons as Alpheus aggressively made adjustments to the charge sheets. The third official asked me if I would not consider Colin's offer. I declined to answer him. I asked if I could get some water but was denied.

We entered the portacabin where two police officers sat. Alpheus presented the charge sheets, whilst the other two sat outside. The officers looked at the charge sheets sternly, then looked at Alpheus suspiciously and glanced at me.

"Is this for real?" the lady officer asked Alpheus as he stood nervously and in front of them. The male officer questioned the validity of the papers.

"This is ridiculous," said the lady officer, whilst her male colleague nodded in approval. There was an exchange of words between them and in the end they stamped the papers and we were on the road again in the sweltering heat.

When we arrived at Chatsworth Courthouse, I barely remember entering the building, my back pain was excruciating and I was weak with hunger and dehydration. When we got inside, I clearly remember seeing my distraught mother and Maureen along with my sister, brother-in-law and family along with my lawyer. He was in and out trying to broker a deal to get me released on bail until a court date was set. We were confident that we would at least achieve that. Colin Bigela and Alpheus Sibila were constantly on their telephones giving the other side a rundown on the proceedings. The tension was rising and time was running out.

Maureen noticed Alpheus Sibila, who had promised to her that he would have me back for the funeral at 1.30pm on the Tuesday. She leapt to her feet to challenge him, but she was overwhelmed with anger and collapsed in front of him. An ambulance was called as my brother-in-law attended to her and when they arrived they gave her oxygen and medical assistance.

My nephew brought me plenty of iced water which was a blessed relief. We later heard that the prosecution was delaying the hearing. At 3.50pm, ten minutes before the court was due to close, the case was called. I entered the dock looking ragged and forlorn, with my family behind me and the three bully boys from Home Affairs seated nearby.

The prosecutor rose to her feet and read out the charges as follows:

1. Remaining in the Republic of South Africa without a visa. *(I was carrying an extended visa, which Habib Khan had obtained during his preliminary work and which we now knew to be false. This was to have been rectified by the Minister of Home Affairs, Mangosuthu Buthelezi as promised by Sadek Mansoor.)*

2. Fraud. *(This was pertaining to the false visa and marriage certificate.)*

3. Corruption. *(This was alleged to be a bribe that I paid a Home Affairs' official, which was ludicrously false and untrue.)*

The Prosecutor occasionally cast a piercing eye in my direction as the judge wrote everything down and at one point complained that he was short of paper. My lawyer, Pregasen Marimuthu, rose to his feet and delivered a strong defence on my behalf. He spoke eloquently and sincerely as he informed the court that I had no convictions in South Africa or anywhere else. He apologised to the court over the lapse in the visa, but said that there were genuine explanations for this and that once the evidence was presented, he felt assured that the court would be satisfied. He produced evidence from the Irish Police, stating that I had no convictions and informed the court that I had brought considerable funds with me to invest in South Africa and to create employment in that country. He also said that I had been defrauded out of all of my money. The black judge interrupted and paused for a moment as he looked at me directly and said, "This is a lengthy argument... are all the witnesses present in court?"

"No. Your Worship," replied the Prosecutor.

"Well, I will have to postpone until Monday," ordered the judge.

The Mansoors had won the day, as it was seen as another delaying tactic.

My lawyer requested that I be set free on bail to the custody of my brother-in-law, a highly respected doctor and medical practitioner, but without warning, the prosecutor jumped to her feet shouting loudly, "Objection, objection! The state objects to bail as the accused is a flight risk. He has no status here in South Africa and we are receiving information that he is involved in a multi-million Rands' syndicate."

I collapsed in the dock and I came through as the emergency services Net Care 911 revived me. They said that I was suffering from a combination of issues; dehydration, lack of food, lack of sleep, tension and shock and that it was imperative that I be hospitalised forthwith.

When I was coherent, I was told by order of the court that I was going to Westville Prison hospital until the hearing on Monday. I was requested to hand the Net Care report to the prison doctor and to stay in bed until Monday morning. I held the written details in my hand on docket number 48507, but the details were never given to any doctor and I was never sent to any hospital.

I parted from my family once again and struggled to get into the prison van in dire pain as I watched the tears run down my mother's face. Maureen and Yvonne sobbed uncontrollably as the Home Affairs officials followed behind. When I disembarked into what I understood to be the grounds of the prison hospital, it was now dark and the three officials approached me again trying to intimidate me. I was limping in a weak state and just wanted to sleep. Colin Bigela repeated his favourite line, "I feel sorry for you. You are NOBODY, a man of insignificance, an alien, once a rich man, now a poor man!"

The shrilling chirping sound of the crickets broke the ominous tension as we walked quietly to an entrance. My self-esteem was at an all-time low and I felt as if I were in the deepest, darkest hell on earth!

My paperwork was completed and I entered what I thought was a hospital. I walked with a nervous member through two sets of doors to a desk in a reception area where once again my fingerprints were taken. We were on the move again, passing by barred cell doors where black prisoners looked in amazement as a white man was being escorted in. We walked through endless corridors, to a cacophony of clanging gates and jeers from prisoners as they looked from behind bars as I wondered where this hospital was.

The member opened a steel door and through open barred gates I could see a multitude of black prisoners squashed together standing shoulder-to-shoulder gazing out at me. They were imprisoned like ill-treated animals. I felt ashamed to be human. This inhumanity deeply affected me and I still think about it to this day. I had been selfishly pitying myself, and here was one hundred and fifty plus human beings caged in what was similar to a pressure cooker and the smell that emanated from the cell was obnoxious beyond comprehension. I asked the member if the doctor would be available so that I could get some medication. I was shocked when he stopped and laughed saying, "What medication? What doctor? You are going to an isolation cell!"

I walked in total despondence, wondering how they could do this. The Court order was ignored and I was exhausted and dehydrated, but I knew in my heart and soul that I could not let them win. Once again my Christian faith came to bear and I prayed for Christ to sustain me.

"Welcome to the VIP suite," said the guard as he opened one outer and one inner door. "I'm privileged," I replied.

I walked into this large open room with no lights whilst the gates slammed behind me. I managed to see my way around, courtesy of the outside lights on the prison road which shone partially through the tiny windows into the cell. I faced in excess of two dozen urine-stained mattresses with cigarette ends and ashes scattered everywhere. The pungent smell was overwhelming. I pulled the best of the bad sponge mattresses over and knew that in order to have strength the following day I needed rest. I fell onto the festering sponge and felt the lice crawling over my skin, but somehow managed to fall asleep through total exhaustion.

The next morning, I arose from my putrid mattress and noticed a large, unhygienic bathroom with bath, shower and toilet along with a minute hand washbasin. It appeared that the place had not been cleaned in a very long time as the place was full of grime and insects. The toilet was clogged and there was no running water.

I lit up a cigarette, walked back inside and had a good look at the room in daylight. There were three sets of window frames, each containing twenty small six inch by twelve inch windows. There were four sets of fluorescent lights on the ceilings. As I wandered around the room, I noticed forty-four floor tiles by thirteen across and two hundred and fifty matching wall tiles. I imagined that this room was quite beautiful when it was originally designed. Despite the dirt, the floor tiles retained a certain quaint beauty. This was to be my home for some sixty hours, without seeing a doctor or receiving any medical assistance.

I was startled by the gurgling of water as it began to flow from the taps in the bathroom. I let the water flow into the filthy bath and leaned over to wash my hair. As I was washing I realised I had no towel, so I took a spare set of socks from my bag and placed them on my hands and dried my hair. It's amazing the resources that you draw on when you are left in a nomadic predicament. I shaved my beard and similarly used my socks to dry my face.

I heard fierce banging as the large security gates swung opened and immediately I was surrounded by inmates from the adjoining cell, mostly teenagers looking for cigarettes. Cigarettes in Westville are like gold dust but dagga is plentiful. However in order for the prisoners to get dagga, they have to pay for it one way or the other! They were all over me like children and I observed their ailments, which consisted of bullet wounds, amputated legs, one of which was still bleeding. There were men who could not walk due to beatings and some who were crippled. There were some with knife stab wounds. Once again I was to see skeletonised men with weeping eyes and vacant expressions, hopelessly dying from AIDS. All in all it was a very depressing state of affairs and it was clear that these people needed proper medical care and hospitalisation. I noticed the outer layers of skin caked on their bodies and when I curiously asked what it was, I was informed that it was "jail lice" from the infested mattresses and blankets. It was the most horrific sight you could imagine on the human body.

It was hard to believe that there were no medical personnel except in the hospital itself and, due to overcrowding, these unfortunates including myself were left on the dumping ground. It was a gross violation of human rights.

A member came in and told me to follow him as I had a visitor. As we walked through the long corridor, I was once again to experience fear and vulnerability as he scared me by telling me the way of life in Westville prison. "This place, man, is run by two factions," he said. "There are hardened criminals who congregate under the title of 'gangs'. These are 26-year-olds and 28-years-old rivals man, bad people; they control the sections with sex, drugs and violence. They would rape you in a flash, especially a white man. The fights man, oh, they are somethin'. One guy bit another guy's ear off the other day and just last night man, a prisoner, he bite the top of a man's penis." He laughed.

I limped and struggled like a Zombie with fear not knowing whether he was for real or a joker in the pack. I was soon to learn with trepidation that the realities of his story were true.

THIRTEEN
Gangs of Evil – Without Fear!

I listened to this burly member telling one tale after the other as we made our way to a visitors' reception area. I envied him as he seemed not to have a care in the world. He was like what we call in Ireland a 'Seanachai', a storyteller.

He continued telling me the story regarding the gangs of evil, without fear! "They even have their own gangs inside this place man; it's hectic. We can only look the other way man, but they pay money, real money man, and this feeds my kids man. Ya know how it is man, real money, yes real money man," he said, licking his lips and swaying his arms to and fro, obviously happy with his arrangement with the prisoners.

Later on, the more research I did and the more I saw convinced me of the induced insanity inside the minds of these ruthless gangs. They were trapped and in order to survive the madness of the jail jungle they used whatever methods they had at their disposal to survive their incarceration. It was a case of a 'dog eat dog' situation and as for the younger inmates it was simply 'monkey see, monkey do!' The power of the 26s and 28s inside Westville Prison extends to all prisons in South Africa and pervades every issue relating to HIV/AIDS in prison. Many high risk behaviours were directly related to gang activity, which includes the rape of other prisoners, unprotected sex, the sharing of needles and tattooing. Membership in both gangs requires frequent tattooing, and it was not uncommon for more than one inmate to be tattooed at a time using the one needle. Violence between prisoners, which also led to bleeding, is also a product of gang activity. Prisoners were required to attack another prisoner and draw blood in order to be initiated into a gang. For membership of the 26s, the practice of stabbing another prisoner, usually a non-gang member, allows the gang member to move up in rank depending on the severity of the attack and the situation of the person who is attacked.

While the 26s engage in stabbings, the primary activity of the 28s is sex and prostitution. The legendary gangs are over 100 years old and take their inspiration from Nongoloza Mathebula, an early Johannesburg thug back in 1906. They originated in the jails, mine compounds and informal settlements and constitute a formidable force in every prison in South Africa. In 1906, the 28s, began to take shape as two loosely connected associations, one inside prison and the other in the mining compounds. Both structures warehoused young men away from their families with minimal opportunities for diversion or normal social interaction. When the gang leader was imprisoned in 1908, he consolidated his criminal empire from his prison base in Pretoria. The prison environment, then and now, providing the ideal location to recruit new members and train them in the tight discipline necessary to maintain gang hierarchical structures.

Although stories vary about the split of the 27s from the 28s, one reason given is the 27s refused to accept the custom of homosexuality, which had become an accepted feature of Nongoloza's gang by that stage.

Nongoloza's gangs were of a unique and staggering brutality, which as seen by me is very much in force today. Its self-styled system, its own judiciaries, sentences inmates to death, to gang rape, to beatings with prison mugs, padlocks and bars of soap contained in socks. Among the prerequisites of joining the 'soldier lines' of the gangs is the taking of a member's or non-gangster's blood. Leaving a prison gang, sharing a gang's secrets with a member, or talking casually about the gang's workings to the non-initiated are all punishable crimes.

The 28s hierarchy consists of two lines, one is the 'men' and the other is their 'wives'. The men do the fighting and protecting and the wives are the sexual partners of the fighters, or men. In addition to being the receptive sexual partner, the wives perform many traditionally considered feminine roles, including washing and other domestic chores. Although the 26s and 27s may claim to eschew homosexual activity and are reportedly forbidden by the gang's official code from taking a wife, staff at Westville Prison, Medium B noted that homosexual activity has become common amongst all gangsters.

According to 'Prison Talk', one former prisoner said that prison wardens or members are also involved in gang activities and gang members will actively recruit prison members as a means of increasing their power. For example, if a prisoner of the 28s wishes to obtain a specific prisoner as a wife, he may be able to gain the complicity of a warden in transferring the targeted prisoner to the gangster's own cell. The former prisoner claimed that the wardens are also known to not only facilitate, but also engage in sexual activities as part of their membership of the gang. The warden's involvement with either the 26s or 28s can also extend to the smuggling in of food, weapons, cigarettes and drugs.

Meanwhile I understood why one prisoner had the ambition to achieve a successful battle with the other, hence the reason for the serious wounds inflicted upon these poor unfortunates awaiting a doctor, who apparently was in no rush to attend to them. They plied their conquests on other prisoners by taking their assigned tea or sugar, or even their meals for sale to other prisoners for cash. The biggest commodity, of course, was cigarettes and these were sold at top dollar in order to secure the weekly supply of dagga from the members. It was vital that their supply was met, otherwise they were faced with rebellion from a very tough and dangerous audience. They would also supply boys to the 28-year-olds for sex and prostitution which was widespread in a frustrated and aggressive prison population.

They watched the kitchen area and dictated who got what, as their trail of followers stole the goods for the purpose of sale. They would steal packages from prisoners who had a visit from family or friends. Those who did not cooperate were subjected to violent beatings, which were not reported to the authorities.

The frequent method of brutality was placing four bars of soap in a sock and beating them over the body or alternatively they used the electric blades to jab their genitals. Worst of all was holding their head in a basin whilst running blunt instruments up the rectum and applying a hot lubricant to inflict as much pain as possible.

The 28-year-olds were more cunning and considered themselves more elite. They liked their dagga and alcohol for personal consumption, as well as selling it to the 26-year-olds who liked to be seen as the 'Stabbing Rambos' of the prison. The 28s had their own share of boys for sex whenever they felt like it. The younger the prisoner the more vulnerable he was to be sodomised by older prisoners. I was told that none of them escaped this brutal rape. There were some who willingly cooperated and engaged in prostitution to save themselves from severe beatings. These transactions were all conducted on a purely commercial basis; in other words prisoners exchanged stolen food from the kitchens or dagga from other prisoners in exchange for sex. They would rob anything they could get their hands on, which caused friction between the gangs, hence the brutal physical warfare. It was common practice for the 28-year-olds to gang rape the 26-years-olds when they did not obey orders. In each camp, there were the Chiefs who were surrounded by their army council, all men doing life imprisonment, which literally meant the rest of their natural lives.

I walked down a long and winding stairwell to the reception, which was ironically immaculate. I was introduced to an officer, who instructed the accompanying member that I was not being sent to the sections. He asked me to sit alone in a private office and less than half an hour later, he entered the office and offered me a cigarette. It was such a relief to enjoy civil company again and I was told it was very unusual for a senior member to offer a prisoner anything.

"Liam," he said, "I am not sending you to the sections of the prison for various reasons, which you need not bother yourself with right now. However, I have no alternative but to leave you upstairs in that room. I know it is bad but at least I will know you are safe. I am told that you will be going home on Monday, which is just as well because I fear for your safety. When I heard of the interested parties in your case, which goes right to the top of public figures in South Africa, I couldn't sleep."

I was startled and confused.

"I find it difficult to explain. You see, should anything happen to you, I am in trouble."

I stared him in disbelief.

"Whatever are you talking about?" I asked.

"You are on my watch and I must protect you from villainous individuals, or shall we say the brutality of the gangs. They are very often influenced from the outside and have been for decades."

I smoked his cigarette as if I were about to face a firing squad. He had his own interests at heart.

"Relax," he said, "Would you like a cup of tea? I've got some English tea if you prefer."

This was like manna from heaven.

"Thank you," I said, as he went on to tell me of his trip to Europe. I seized the opportunity in this brief hour of friendship and asked if I could use the telephone to call my family and he not only agreed but allowed them to visit me as well. They brought me bottled water, juices, fruits, snacks, pens and pencils and a writing pad along with fresh clothing. I was still in agony with back pain and headaches and here I was in this large cell with no medication or doctor, a matter that was later raised in court but ignored. It was insanity beyond belief.

In the early afternoon of Saturday 27 April 2002, the outer and inner doors to the room were opened by a member who never said a word and disappeared as quickly as he arrived. It was an eerie feeling and when I started to gather up my empties, I heard someone behind me. As I turned I noticed that this black guy had entered wearing pyjamas covered in stained blood. His hands were behind his back and he requested a cigarette. I looked at him and noticed that he had only one eye. He had a large scar that ran down to his cheekbone.

"I'm sorry!" I replied somewhat confused. He immediately released his hands from behind his back and waved a long nailed stick with which he attempted to swipe at me. I jumped onto the soiled flea-infected mattresses with my attacker in pursuit, but when I rolled off them, I jumped to my feet and picked up one of the sponge mattresses to protect myself. I noticed him struggling. This gave me the upper hand to disarm him on the floor. I looked at the stick with its piercing nails, which was enough to kill me or leave me permanently maimed. I threw it through one of the small barred windows as two other inmates from the adjoining cell rushed to my rescue and physically removed him. They returned within minutes to enquire after my wellbeing and pleaded that the incident should not be reported to the authorities. They said that they would all be punished but that if I agreed, they would deal with the guy themselves. He was a schizophrenic killer and his presence left me cold and uneasy. I agreed under the circumstances and tried to forget the ordeal, which was practically impossible. I struggled with back pain after my brief unexpected encounter with this inmate. The loneliness and fear was crippling. Once more, the gates were locked and once more I was alone, but safe, or so I thought.

I piled the mattresses on top of each other, so that I could sit comfortably whilst I could continue making notes for my records. I wanted to keep a diary of all the events so as not to forget anything. It was a case of occupational therapy. I was nearing completion of the third page, when I heard the gates opening. A tall Indian member stood looking down at me.

"What are you doing?" he asked, whilst fixing his trouser belt.

"I'm having a bath! What does it look like?" I retorted as he approached me.

"Let me see the papers," he demanded.

"Do you have a court order?" I asked as he grabbed the papers from me and began to read.

"Forgive me, I was not aware that it was against regulations to write," I said whilst watching him read my notes.

"Nobody is allowed to write like this whilst in prison," he said.

"Why? Are you afraid of the truth? Or is it that you are ashamed of it?"

I looked at him more closely and said, "Surely you above all people remember the harshness of the apartheid years less than a decade ago. Why can you not just ignore this?"

"You watch yourself or I'll have you," he said chillingly, as he stared at me and flung the papers on the floor as he hastily made a noisy exit.

What next? I thought.

It was now nearing nightfall and the only light that was now operational was in the bathroom. I took a towel out of my bag and placed it on the toilet seat, where I sat for several hours writing until I felt tired. I went to sleep thinking about what had transpired during the day as the parasites crawled from the mattress covering my entire body.

I woke on Sunday 28 April 2002 and 24 hours before the Court hearing, which I had believed would result in my release. The gates opened with the usual clanging and, despite being warned by the members, the inmates strolled casually in and out of my cell, two of whom asked me to help them write to their families. I wondered why they should bother as I feared they would never reach their destination but their enthusiasm was sparkling.

I was looking out the window onto the long and winding road that led to an exit in the distance and I was hoping that within twenty-four hours this would be my path to freedom. There were two giant chimney stacks in the distance and a crane used for carrying goods. I saw those chimney stacks as my pillars of strength and the crane like the bird about to fly freely away. They were comforting thoughts on that lonely Sabbath day.

A man who was 29 years old, but looked like a man of later years, beckoned to join me. He was stooped and barely able to walk. He introduced himself as Amos and struggled desperately to catch his breath. He reminded me of the veterans we see in movies from the Vietnam War, a sad and pathetic sight. It was difficult for me to understand what he was saying but other inmates helped him to tell me his story. He alleged that the South African police had beaten him with batons and that he was awaiting trial for assault. He winced in agony as it took him five minutes to walk the length of the room. He took several breaths before speaking, but this was due to the brutal beatings and it appeared that he had a chest infection. The jail lice covered his whole body.

The sun was shining fiercely through the six barred but open windows and onto the disgusting grounds below. They were littered with papers, cans and bones from the nearby kitchens and there was an open filthy sewer infested with rats that scurried to and fro. As the heat drained my energy, I made an acquaintance with a proud Muslim named Shah who tried to engage me in a conversation regarding Islam. In the course of the conversation, he informed me that he was a cook and that he had served fifteen years for armed robbery, but he was due for release within seven days. He boasted how he would enjoy the fruits of his ill-gotten gains of one million rands he had stolen fifteen years earlier. I later heard that upon his release he went in search of the money to find that he had been double crossed and he committed suicide.

A member came rushing in shouting for everyone to get out and at 2pm the gates were once again locked. I decided to have my last bottle of water, but my fruit was gone and I went without food for another day. My back pain was worsening and the strain of not having a chair to sit on exacerbated the pain. I continued to write until dusk when I retired to my office (the filthy unhygienic bathroom), where I had the benefit of the light bulb and the toilet bowl as my seat.

There was a sudden rattle at the door as I heard the sound of keys and the lock turning. I once again hid my notes and went to investigate the disturbance. It was an Indian member who earlier had refused to allow me to use the telephone to call my family. He gave no reason why, but allowed everyone else within the wing to use the phone. He had looked me up and down with a callous smirk, but I refused to let him see that I was annoyed.

He was quite a heavy chap, but his femininity outshone his job description. He reminded me of a drag queen as he stood in the shadow and I asked him what he wanted. He remained silent and didn't answer my question, but instead he lit up a cigarette and stood with his back against the wall. The silence was broken by the occasional sound of a van driving inside the large prison grounds and then a jet zoomed overhead as he finally spoke.

"Like to be on that?"

There was silence once again in the stillness of the night. I looked at him through the haze of cigarette smoke and hesitated before replying, "Anything would be better than this."

"Anything?" he retorted.

I knew instinctively where he was heading.

"Yes, anything out of this vile cesspit," I replied.

He dragged on his cigarette and replied, "Oh come now, what more can you ask for? You have a private room and you have me," grabbing his crotch as he spoke.

"I think the former will suffice for now, thank you," I replied.

"I'm offering it to you on a golden platter," he replied.

"No thank you," I insisted.

He minced towards me, blowing his cigarette smoke in my direction. I became nervous and backed up towards the window.

"What are you playing at?" I asked.

He grabbed hold of my hair and pulled my head towards him. As I struggled to break loose, he held my head in the grip of his arm and tried earnestly to kiss me as his fat face and bulging lips smothered me. I could smell intense garlic from his breath as he tried to put his tongue in my mouth. I began to have a panic attack and my heart was pounding as he pushed his crotch against my leg. I was trapped and in the shadow of the bathroom light, I could see his alarmingly intense wild eyes as he struggled to open his trousers. He pulled my head towards his penis and demanded an oral job, but I fell with back pain unconscious against a ledge. I cannot remember anything other than awakening naked to find him engaged in a sexual act with another inmate, a slightly retarded crippled prisoner who seemed delighted with his experience.

I realised how physically fit the effeminate and chubby prison officer was after he had wrestled and attacked me. I was no match for his strength. Realising that I was semi-conscious, he began slapping me across the face and I could feel the rush of blood to my head, churning inside as if it were a kettle reaching boiling point. The pain was unbearable. I prayed that he would leave me alone, but he bent down, took his belt from his trousers lying on the floor and hit me with it as the other inmate giggled in hysterics. I felt the pounding of the buckle against my back and shoulders and I pleaded with him to stop. I was drifting in and out of consciousness and, in a final act of brutality, he beckoned his prisoner companion to urinate on my naked body. He did so in an almost insane fit, breathing heavily with an uncontrollable whimper of laughter. In hindsight, it was like a spine-chilling episode from an Alfred Hitchcock presentation and to this very day the face of that camp, but callous, evil prison member and the smell of his garlic is still with me.

He was carrying out his fetish by using a prisoner with mental and physical disorders who obviously enjoyed the favouritism, but somehow I felt that it would not be long before the member would be swapping his warden's uniform for the reeking green tunic that the prisoners called their suit of clothes. He was the most revolting man I have ever had the misfortune to meet and that gruelling experience of violation gave me an insight into what the victims of rape are subjected to by deviants.

I had been violated and abused by a man who had the trait of a deranged and lethal predator, a warden in a notorious prison in a newly elected democratic black state abusing all the power entrusted upon him. It was his duty to care for the prisoners, but he chose to exercise his perverse ways and would question the sanity of his position in an already dubious place of detention. It was hell on earth and South Africa's shame.

I was distressed and frightened, but as the member dressed, his sidekick walked over and spat on me, all the time laughing hideously. The member told me to get dressed and to say nothing or else, blowing a kiss as he left. Once again the gate banged, slammed and closed and I selfishly prayed that I would pass away in my sleep.

FOURTEEN
A Glimpse of Depravity

At 4.30am on 29 April 2002, the day of my court appearance, I turned on the taps so that I would hear the gurgling of water when they turned it on. One hour later the gurgling commenced, followed by the free flow of water. Following a wash, I took hold of my notes, tucked it safely into my only towel and placed it beneath my other belongings. I was anxious to get the hearing over and done with so that I could travel back to Ireland with my mother and Maureen. I was suffering the terrible effects of the night before, with extreme emotional, physical pain and a pounding headache.

The time appeared to go very slowly and there was no sign of the officials from the Department of Home Affairs arriving to take me to court. At 7.50am a senior member, accompanied by three of his companions entered and said, "Why are you not in the waiting area?"

I looked at him and said, "Do I look like I am in possession of keys?"

I was taken down to the waiting area and told to wait outside a large caged area, where over two hundred black and Indian prisoners were awaiting transportation to the courts. Our names were called in bunches of twenty and I complained that it was very late, since I was scheduled to meet my lawyer at 9am and it was now 8.50am. I was told that there was no sign of the officials from Home Affairs and the police refused to take me. I asked if I could use the telephone but was refused and when I asked for a drink of water I was, as always, refused.

It was now a week before I had eaten properly apart from the fruit on Saturday. I noticed the prisoner who had engaged in sexual activity with the member the night before, hobbling along a side corridor with a bucket of water and a mop cleaning the floor and nervously watching my every move snidely. The saliva from his mouth dribbled upon his cracked lips and his eyes shifted in all directions as if he was about to fly into a fierce rage. He gazed at me occasionally, pretending to play with himself and laughed eerily exposing his broken teeth and the discharge from his nose drooled disgustingly down his face.

The member, from the night before appeared making sure that no one from the office saw him, as he warned me, "Keep quiet or it will get worse!"

I did not reply, but I stared at him as he worked in order to intimidate him.

I sensed that something was wrong and no one was prepared to tell me anything. It was now 9.20am, so I asked a member who said, "I'm fed up with all of this."

I was surprised at his outburst and asked him to explain his concern, but he ignored me. Within minutes, he returned to say the police would take me and as he delivered the message, he looked all around and said, "Just be careful." I was living on a knife edge!

I was led out to the awaiting police wagon with eight others already present and tossed the statement from the member over and over in my mind, but concluded that there was no point in worrying about it, difficult as it was. Over the weekend, one of the prisoners had said to me that he found it strange that people only turn to God when they are in trouble. I turned to God to help me to get out of the quagmire, because I was physically strained and had little energy to fend off potential attackers. I climbed into the wagon extremely tired, as weary prisoners tried to make room for me. The stench of their body bacteria was stifling in the heat of the morning sun. The wagon rumbled down the road as it made its way to Chatsworth Court and I too prayed for a good result and freedom from the nightmare I was experiencing. The nerves in my stomach churned and tightened and my head pounded in pain as we drove over lumps and bumps to an unknown fate in a South African court, seeking justice for crimes for which I was not responsible.

My faith in the Mother of God was always strong but, like a beggar, I had to plead with her to help me to escape from a dubious and perilous situation, which was way beyond imaginable proportions. This horrendous place was in time to provide me with a life-changing experience.

I later learned that the officials from the department of Home Affairs were instructed not to collect me from Westville Prison, so that the case would not be heard on that day, 29 April, and that there would be no need for an adjournment. This was another delaying tactic by the Mansoors, giving them extra time to prepare false statements and persuade people to perjure themselves in court. They were in no rush to have the case heard at all. It was through the mercy of God that the astute member was willing to help me get to the court and it was he who asked a police friend to take me with the others.

As usual the intense heat was stifling in the prison wagon as it made its journey, often stopping at shops for the officers to buy their ice-cold juices. I watched every drop they swallowed as my throat was like a cement pit and my clothes were drenched in perspiration, as we sat sandwiched together. I once again felt tremendously weak and listless with my back pain worsening. I have travelled in many luxury modes of transport in my time, but this was akin to torture as the sun beat down relentlessly. I was desperately alone and wondered why this was happening to me and why I was not receiving help from those in authority.

We arrived at Chatsworth Court in the suburbs of Durban and were led to the cells beneath the courthouse. As usual, I was the only white person amongst the one hundred or so blacks and Indians in this one caged cell, which had an adjoining cell next to it. I shared the dungeon with a plethora of thugs and drug addicts, anticipating a violent row as tempers soared between them over who stole a supply from whom. I surveyed the grimy walls, decorated with slogans and graffiti of a derogatory nature, referring to various prisoners as 'Mother Cunts'.

The police arrived back and took out eighty prisoners, leaving me with the remaining twenty or so. They were very intimidating and although I was scared, I attempted to shrug it off as I had no choice. They looked at me with suspicious eyes and uttered snide remarks and, in hindsight, I do not know where I obtained my strength.

My brother-in-law Naren and my lawyer Pregasen arrived in subdued moods as they informed me that Westville Prison was not cooperating with the Irish Embassy in Pretoria. Whilst they repeatedly asked about my well-being and general welfare, they had called to organise papers for my return to Ireland, but were receiving no information whatsoever. In view of the fact that my passport had been confiscated, they were preparing an emergency passport so that I could fly home the next day with my mother and Maureen. It transpired that Sadek Mansoor wanted me out of the country to avoid embarrassment whilst Ahmed Yacoob wanted me to stay in prison to break my spirit, force me to succumb to defeat and not take any proceedings against them.

"The longer he stays there, the more likely he will return a broken man to Ireland," he would muse.

The pressure was mounting on the Mansoors from the very top, as questions were being asked by the Irish Embassy, concerned over my safety. Then there followed a dramatic twist to events as Sadek Mansoor contacted my brother-in-law and said he would see to it that I was safely put on a plane if I agreed to be escorted from prison the following day. In an exhausted state of mind and for the sake of my family, especially my mother, I agreed, even though I was innocent, I couldn't cope anymore. I was assured that it would be better to fight them in the comfort and safety of my own country than from some stinking cell at Westville Prison, where I would have little or no hope.

Suddenly, my lawyer took the steps in threes as he descended from the court room in a total rage.

"They say they have more information alleging that you are involved with criminal organisations in this country. Is there anything I should know?" he said in a trembling voice.

"This is absolutely absurd, why don't you get my family and many friends here in South Africa into the dock who will testify that I never did anything wrong. I am the victim here, I am the one who has been robbed, beaten and mugged."

For a split second, I thought they had infiltrated the one man we trusted.

I was shocked. He saw the consternation on my face and said apologetically, "Sorry Liam for the knee-jerk reaction."

"What on God's earth are they talking about?" I exclaimed. "I am never going to get out of here, am I?"

Pregasen, looking as dejected as I did, returned to the courtroom for further discussion. I was incensed, since it was clear we were dealing with Mafia-style individuals and each hour seemed to be getting us nowhere. It was way beyond belief that a man in a wheelchair, incapacitated from the neck down and having been nursed back to life by my brother-in-law, following a boating accident, was conspiring and committing such a despicable act of deceit, lies, theft, thuggery and violation of decent human trust and friendship.

Pregasen later returned to inform me that he had seen documents with my alleged signature, indicating that I was part of a multi-million fraud operation. This was in time proven to be fraudulent and had no substance in it whatsoever, simply because it was not true. I needn't tell you the mind boggled. They were clutching at straws and panicking. Ahmed Yacoob Mansoor double-crossed Sadek; hence any potential deal of release became null and void. Ahmed Mansoor was running scared of a civil lawsuit that I might take against him and his only escape was for me to be 'banged up', as he was alleged to have said for a long time.

The police told me that the Mansoors had placed the Minister for Home Affairs, Mangosuthu Buthelezi in the most crucial and frustrating position of his long political life. However, this did not deter the Mansoors, as they wriggled like a snake out of their dilemma. They had a lawsuit for a multi-million rands involving a dubious syndicate unknown to me which was a very serious worry to them both. In the meantime, they wanted someone removed from office in the Home Affairs' department, who was apparently an obstacle to progress. It would have been to their delight if I had agreed to testify against this man, whom they were to say that I bribed for the extension to my visa. I had never met the man in my life, apart from the day of my arrest on 23 April 2002, when he was introduced to me as Terence Menthe. Menthe was later to fall on his own sword.

It was difficult to know at times whether I was coming or going with the considerable indecisions, all pertaining to my release. The judge had to be informed of this unreliable, fictitious string of allegations and the prosecution was sternly ordered to produce the evidence to a higher court by 06 May 2002. The matter was then transferred to 'K' court in the city of Durban's regional district. The court informed me that I was to be held at Chatsworth police station for a week. My mother and Maureen postponed their flight to Ireland for a while.

In the meantime I inadvertently overheard Alpheus Sibila saying to Colin Bigela, "It's not going our way. I'd better let them know."

I was then led into a cell of one hundred reprobates waiting to be taken back to Westville. There I was robbed of cigarettes whilst the inmates also stripped one big Indian guy of all his jewellery, phone cards and a snake trouser belt. They even made one prisoner drop his pants as others looked up his rectum for concealed drugs. This led to a fist fight and one inmate suffering a split lip.

We were kept there for 90 minutes and the leader of the ruthless gang became restless and eyed various vulnerable individuals before jumping on a young twenty-year-old, aided by five others. He was dragged into a corner behind a crowd, where they pulled his pants down and raped him repeatedly. Although gagged, I could hear his weakened cries for help but everyone ignored his distress in fear of their own lives. When it was over, the young man stood up shaking and with tears in his eyes, he fixed his clothing. No words were spoken and no one asked questions. I simply could not comprehend these vicious sadistic actions that were happening before my very eyes. Weeks later, I saw one of the young rapists, who chatted to me and cried like a baby after been sentenced to twelve years' imprisonment for another offence. There was no sign of the 'macho' image that day, only a pathetic human being.

It was time for them to go to Westville prison and I did not envy them, but I was relieved when they left and the station sergeant offered me a cigarette. He and a colleague walked me to the station, which was around the corner. I noticed Mansoor in the distance sitting in the passenger seat of a car chatting to Home Affairs officials, but they did not expect to see me walking out with a police officer who, it might be said, had one or two drinks in the course of his day's work and fell into a pot hole in the ground. I could now see the enemy lurking in the wings and felt a sense of disquiet. The officer composed himself and we were on our way to the cells at Chatsworth police station.

I was taken into a 60 x 15 foot dimly lit cell where a painting of the Madonna adorned the back wall. It was a welcome change from the filth, graffiti and excrement of previous experiences. There were six black prisoners present, five of whom were from Durban and one from Kenya. The Kenyan had severe bruising on his arms and legs, with head injuries consistent with heavy blows or severe beatings. He wore a bloodstained kaftan and his eyes were bulging from his head, but he was still and silent, as if he were approaching death's door. The night was devoted to getting to know each other and regaling interesting tales about Mandela and Mbeki. (Taboo Mbeki, was then President of the Republic of South Africa.)

My distraught mother and sister Yvonne came to see me but were not allowed to bring any food. The pain that my mother was bearing was clearly perceptible on her face. She was being strong for all of us, as any mother would be for her children. The Irish spirit, although strong within us, called for support and if ever we needed the support of all the saints of Ireland we needed them that night. It was emerging that the family home in Durban had been bugged and the telephone lines were tapped. My family had brought in experts and complained to the Minister, but there was no action taken.

The Department of Home Affairs sent officials to our family home in Durban to search for illegal refugees, another ploy in the twisted minds of the Mansoors who persuaded their thuggish friends to intimidate the family. They suggested that we were harbouring 'aliens', anything to upset us, but more importantly it was part of their game plan to distort justice. We continued with faith in our hearts and determination not to succumb to their threats and intimidation, but with the physical back pain, malnutrition and mental torture I was enduring, it was a relief at the end of each day to lie on a hard mat to relieve some of the pain and attempt to sleep.

I heard prisoners being intimate with each other when there was a quick scuffle as they leapt under a blanket beneath the painting of the Madonna. It was 2.30am when a drunken Indian guy was led into the cell and then another man entered accused of hijacking a car on the highway. In light of these disturbances I knew that I would not be able to sleep. I began to experience chest pains and lay flat on my back as my mind drifted in all directions. I could hear the noise of the cockroaches in the silence of the night and the beautiful sound and humming of the birds in the early morning sunlight. My emotions were everywhere.

In prison in 2002, my life seemed fruitless and my self-esteem was all but destroyed as I logically tried to comprehend in which direction South Africa was going. The years of oppression by the white minority and the long suffering years of Nelson Mandela seemed futile to the actions of the corrupt officials and leaders, who were recklessly destroying that legacy. Mangosuthu Buthelezi had refused to answer mail I had sent to him, but I feared he may not have received it. However, after my release he still refused to acknowledge my predicament and denied knowing the Mansoors which was economical with the truth.

At 7am, the gate to the cell was finally opened, which led into a small wet yard for exercise and an open shower against the wall. The day was dull and gloomy with intermittent rain showers. The Kenyan was in tremendous pain and I helped him to stand up. My own legs were weak, my back pain was worse and I had dreadful chest pains, I decided to lie down until my family came to visit. They were horrified at my appearance and complained bitterly to the desk sergeant that I was ill and needed treatment. The night of 30 April, I was shifted under armed guard to Chatsmed Gardens Hospital to a general ward. A complete examination took place and it was deemed necessary for me to remain in hospital. I was given a strong sedative and slept soundly.

On 01 May 2002, I was shifted to a private ward under the supervision of three armed guards who worked in shifts of eight hours each. A masseuse was assigned at our expense on a daily basis to treat my back pain and doctors and nurses came routinely, including my brother-in-law in his capacity as a doctor. They were very concerned over my weight loss, but I slowly began eating again and the hospital authorities and their staff were very kind to me. I was allowed visitors and walks in the gardens, always followed by my guard, but the sense of freedom was gratifying. I knew that I would never be reimbursed and the hospital costs were enormous.

On Saturday 04 May 2002, my guard told me that there was a gentleman from the department of Home Affairs present to take some more details, including my fingerprints. The guard remained outside the ward talking to another officer as Alpheus Sibila entered, as usual perspiring profusely. He always reminded me of a man who was working against his principles although he was arrogant and unsympathetic.

"Am I making you nervous Mr Sibila?" I asked.

As he placed his items on the bed he pulled his gun in a threatening pose, leaned towards me and said, "The message I have for you is to plead guilty and get out of this country; if you do not cooperate, the consequences for you and your family will be dire. We will take no nonsense from any of you and this we swear. You wouldn't like anything to happen to your mother or that bullying old lady who attacked me, would you?"

In a shocked state I remained silent, but what was abundantly clear to me was that these were no idle threats and they would carry out executions if I did not cooperate. As he prepared swiftly and nervously to take my fingerprints, the door opened suddenly and the hospital security entered scolding Alpheus Sibila for leaving the reception area without clearance of his firearms. They ordered him never to bring his weapons into the hospital again and demanded that he hand them over, but a deviant Sibila informed the security officer that he was a government official and would carry his gun where he liked. They argued at length, with Sibila taking the fingerprints on the wrong page and my guard showing him what to do. On completion, he left abruptly with the guard speaking privately to him. I had my suspicions and when the guard returned he said to me, "They want to handcuff you to the bed with no further exercises, but I told him he would have to check with my boss."

This never transpired and I was never handcuffed at any stage during the ordeal but I was extremely concerned and anxious over his threats.

The department of Home Affairs were now getting awkward over extending a visa to my mother and Maureen, so they decided to return to Ireland because of the threats and the tenuous situation to which they were subjected to. So, on 05 May 2002, I had to say goodbye reluctantly to my mother and Maureen as they left for Ireland. They were completely distraught and looked significantly older than their years. I wondered if I would ever see them again.

On 06 May, two armed guards arrived into the hospital to take me to 'P' court in the centre of Durban to meet with the eminent Advocate Mr Jimmy Howse, who was going to represent me in court. Mr Howse was a prominent barrister and a former magistrate. He was extremely experienced in his field and we got on very well together. I declined to inform Mr Howse about Alpheus Sibila and his threats, as I was genuinely scared that something sinister might occur, but I did inform him of Colin Bigela seeking 6,000 rands (£600 in those days) to set me free.

The matter was adjourned until 08 May and I was taken to the cells below the court in icy conditions. I did not arrive back at the hospital until 9pm that night, a full five hours late. I would have been there longer had it not been for my brother-in-law reporting me as missing. The guards verbally abused me and incited other prisoners to intimidate me, a shocking ordeal that we heard was a directive by the Mansoors. They had their lackeys everywhere in police stations and prisons. The matter was a cause of confrontation in the court later in the week. I was freezing cold on arrival at the hospital and the nursing staff knew what was going on. They went out of their way to protest to the guards of my ill treatment. The officers were unconcerned. I remember the affection of one black nurse who said she would pray for me and her simple sentiments filled my heart with strength.

On 07 May, I was handed a newspaper article concerning Ahmed Yacoob Mansoor, who was seeking an interdict against our friend Shaun and me, along with my brother-in-law Naren. It had been lodged with the High Court on 30 April 2002 and contained an outrageous list of lies, false statements and language that was unbecoming of all three of us. He presented himself as a puritan and was seeking all kinds of damages in excess of the 600,000 rands (£60,000 in those days) he already owed me, in order to give himself legal weight in the event of a civil action being taken against him. He was trying to cover all of his tracks and fraudulent deeds. It refrained from detailing the applicant's attorney, only to say 'Amod's Attorney' at 900 Nedbank House. This was the address for Zayed Paruk of Lockhat & Associates who had drafted up our mutual unsigned agreement. They were seen as devious and sinister, with a dismal reputation in Durban. In later months, we heard that an associate attorney of Mansoors had been sent to prison. This was not surprising as they were a ruthless family and anyone who crossed them, irrespective of their position, was admonished accordingly.

The interdict order sought to prohibit us from assaulting or harassing Ahmed and said he was acting on behalf of a person by the name of 'Sadek', leaving out the surname by association and making it look good, or so he thought! He said the deal in Cape Town went sour because I refused to hand over the transfer costs and he claimed that I threatened him with follow-up calls from my brother-in-law and Shaun and that he felt scared and intimidated which was absurd. He went further by saying that I had telephoned his attorney and said that if his client did not pay me the money he owed me that I would see to it that "every drop of his blood was shed". It made fascinating reading, almost like a Mafia novel and the Indian community to whom it was targeted as readers poured scorn on this villainous rogue and suggested he should write novels for a living.

The application was received and registered with the courts, but was never heard until the matter was raised at my hearing and later at the Court of Appeal when they dismissed it out of hand and said, "It was a clear attempt to blackmail the appellant."

There were never violent or abusive threats made by any of our party, only the fearful threats made by these sinister gangsters. Ahmed Mansoor failed to mention in his affidavit that all funds had been fraudulently obtained including the transfer fees, but conveniently said it was a commission for Sadek who had originally said he was negotiating the deal as a favour to Naren for saving his life. The deal was never completed, as Ahmed stole the money, as he had also done with other monies belonging to me and never paid the transfer fees already in his possession. I am quite sure that his attorneys never said what he had alleged, but rather the evil Ahmed was conjuring up stories late at night whilst playing with his PC.

Mansoor continued intimidating business adversaries as reported in the press until a High Court judge caught up with him and evicted him out of his premises, owned by insurance giant Sanlam, less than a year after the Appeal Court judges admonished them in my case. They said that the wrath of the law ought to be turned on those responsible for my predicament and incarceration.

On 08 May, just prior to the court hearing, Alpheus Sibila viciously reminded me of what I had to do, otherwise the consequences would be brutal. In the absence of my mother, my family were now vulnerable to harm. My body was swamped with tranquilisers and I was not fully compos mentis.

In the meantime, back at the court I was informed that the judge and prosecutor were Muslim and my whole life fell apart. The prosecutor, a young tiny lady with prominent teeth, was one who excited herself towards the public gallery, unlike Mr Howse who professionally played to the court with the facts and not fiction. The magistrate, who it was alleged was a friend to the Mansoors, had been well briefed on the case. It was said from the very start from many people that we would not get a fair hearing. A police officer at the hospital who was affiliated to guard duties alleged that the magistrate "was on the take."

The nerve-racking moment arrived as the clerk stood and the burly magistrate Ms Mohamed took her centre-stage seat on the bench. Her eyes were pierced on her private papers and she greeted no one. She sat for a while, eyes down with an almost guilty expression on her face, which I found puzzling. After about ninety seconds, she nodded to the goofy prosecutor, who told her that it was an application for the accused to remain at Chatsmed hospital and not Westville Prison.

The application proceeded as Mr Howse called my brother-in-law, Naren, who was sworn in before the cross examination commenced. It had now been established that we had been brothers-in-law for the past 24 years and that Naren was a graduate of the National University of Ireland and also a general and consultant medical practitioner. The incident in Chatsworth Court where I collapsed and was ordered to hospital was discussed. He told the court that I was suffering with hypoglycaemia and dehydration and clarified that I had not been taken to the prison hospital as ordered but to a private ward at enormous expense four days later, under the services of another doctor, Usha Shri Kissoon. Mr Howse asked Naren on his opinion of my fitness to be sent to Westville Prison and he replied, "Well, it is my professional opinion that whatever we have achieved to date will be jeopardised if he is sent to Westville."

Mr Howse thanked him and the prosecutor rose to her feet, gripping her pen. She looked at the public gathered in the courtroom and, in a piercing voice, directed her question at Naren, "Sir, what did you say was the physical problem with the accused?" Naren looked sternly at her and replied, "He was a passenger in a car accident some years ago and suffers back pain, Mr Amra Khan, a physiotherapist at the hospital is looking after him."

She went on, needlessly arguing over medical conditions of which she was clearly not qualified, and further suggested that there was something devious going on at the hospital, because they had to wait a considerable time for me on the previous Monday. I was under armed guard for five hours and locked up under her nose on the previous Monday, but she accused me of wandering home whenever I felt like it, which received gasps of laughter and disbelief in the courtroom. She was becoming more annoyed by the minute, but a feeding line from the Home Affairs was to grab the attention of the court as she said, "Sir, what about the allegation, that (the state will lead evidence of that) the investigating officers did not even have the opportunity to see the accused in Chatsmed Hospital and that—"

There was an intervention by Mr Howse, "Objection, objection!"

She stared aggressively at him as the magistrate said, "Continue Miss Prosecutor."

She took a deep breath and continued, "They were even prevented from just seeing his face, not that they wanted to talk to him at Chatsmed Hospital. Sir, are you aware of this?"

"No, I am not," replied Naren.

"Okay, what about the allegation that the accused was returning home at night from Chatsmed Hospital, going to his home in Mobeni Heights?"

"That is untrue."

"How do you know it's untrue Sir?"

"The last day we were here, the decision was taken to transfer him back to Chatsmed Hospital. He was taken from here to the cells below and the impression I got was that he was going straight back, but instead he was held here for five hours whilst our attorney phoned all the prisons in the Durban area. He is sick; he is supposed to be in bed."

The prosecutor rearranged her attire and staring at the judge she said, "So, who then took him back to hospital?"

"Upon making enquiries to find out whether he ended up in Chatsworth Prison or CR Swart Prison or Westville Prison again, we made enquiries to all three. We finally got information that he was left in a freezing cold cell here at CR Swart. We demanded that he be taken back to the hospital, but instead he was taken back to Chatsworth where another escort took him back to hospital."

She banged her desk in front and said, "Your Worship, it appears that no one has control over the accused, not even the doctor who cannot control the patient's whereabouts and…"

There were further bouts of laughter, driving her into a frenzy as she was basically misleading herself and no one had any idea what she was trying to say. She tried to implicate Naren, and out of family loyalty he was keeping me at the hospital. He retorted by suggesting she call the other doctors involved but she declined. She ended her cross-examination by becoming confused with her days and referring to the police when she meant prison guards and vice versa. It was established that the driver would at all times guarantee my safe journey to and from the hospital punctually, a matter that could have been settled instantaneously.

The prosecutor was still not happy and called Vala Prabashan Naidoo, Chief Immigration Officer from the Department of Home Affairs, whom she cross-examined with Mr Howse. She asked the officer to tell the court what problems his department had in locating me in the hospital and the alleged frustrations his members had in taking me to court and making sure the police were doing their job. This man stood before the court and said, "We have received calls that, in fact, he was not at Chatsmed at all times and that he was, in fact, seen at another destination in Chatsworth. To verify this, I sent the two investigating officers to the hospital to clarify that he was there and they stipulated that he was, but they were refused point blank to see the accused in his ward at all."

She asked about delays in getting me to the court and he replied, "Ma'am, once the accused is in the custody of

SAPS [South African Police Services], he is under their jurisdiction and therefore we must make arrangements on our own. Now since we have no jurisdiction over him and he is on a court docket, we were unable to do so. Fortunately, we got members from the Organised Crime Unit, who were willing to try and help in this process, but a member from the Border Police was contacted who was near the station, which was near the hospital and he, in fact, brought the accused to court."

Jimmy Howse stood and looked pensively at Mr Naidoo, who seemed a little apprehensive of the Advocate as he calmly asked him, "Mr Naidoo, the difficulty in establishing where the accused was, which ward he was in; that, I take it, was not today?"

"No Sir," he replied. (He trembled and excused himself before he gave a light cough.)

"That was the last occasion?"

"That is correct."

Mr Howse put the nervous officer at ease and said, "Okay that was Monday and today there was no difficulty and the problem with the police has been resolved?"

Looking drawn and directly at Jimmy Howse, Naidoo said, "That is correct."

Thinking that his examination was over, Naidoo was about to leave when suddenly the learned Advocate spurned a series of fast questions at him, sometimes showing anger at his lack of spontaneous answers, but at the same time clearing the air and establishing the facts. He then paused, looked at the magistrate and then across to Vala Naidoo and said, "The information you have, or have received, I presume is from reliable sources; it's not something that one of your investigators actually saw with their own eyes, or is it?"

Wiping his forehead he replied, "Well, this was an informer who told our department about it."

Mr Howse looked at him derisively and said, "An informer?"

"Yes," replied Naidoo.

With a vehement look, the eminent barrister turned to the magistrate and said, "Your Worship, I have nothing further."

There was silence in the courtroom as the crumbled officer left the witness box, clearly defeated on his weak and unreliable admission.

There were continuing arguments between Mr Howse and the prosecutor, who was intent on sending me to Westville Prison. She expressed her annoyance that they were not allowed extra time to investigate the alleged syndicate, which was fabricated, and basically made a show of herself, stating that I was not at the hospital, when I was under armed guard at all times.

All they had to do was to summon the station sergeant in charge of my police guards and the matron or a spokesperson for the hospital to verify or eliminate her doubts, but instead she purposely wasted time and went on accusing and at times using tones not dissimilar to that of the Mansoors themselves.

The magistrate reluctantly delivered her ruling and said, "Mr Ledwidge, with regards to where you are going to stay from today until Friday, I have listened to the evidence of the doctor and I do understand that you have a medical problem. I am not going to interfere with the doctor's instructions that you be kept at a certain hospital. The matter is adjourned until Friday. It is just a day away and in the circumstances, I will order that you be kept, once again, at Chatsmed Gardens Hospital pending the finalisation of this case on Friday."

Once again, I returned to the cells below and because of the incident on Monday, it appeared there were to be no delays that day. The police were waiting for me, but before we left, we chatted and had a cigarette. However in the course of the conversation, a guard informed me that he had overheard the prosecutor speaking several times to the Mansoors and it was their tactics that were being fed to her to delay the matter. She was viewed as an expensive puppet on a string.

I was optimistic about the outcome of the forthcoming hearing as the Mansoors were very influential and had everyone in their pockets as corruption was and is endemic in South Africa. Despite its faults, I knew I would miss my beloved South Africa, a country where I had so many beloved memories from my many trips and dreams as a child of visiting that part of Africa. Having conquered that dream, I enjoyed the land with its diverse cultures and its gregarious people which was now shattered. I once felt that all South Africans could be proud of their land, with a man the whole world was in awe of, Nelson Mandela. My fate was now in the hands of a suspicious magistrate named Fariedha Mohammed who, like the Mansoors, I could not trust.

FIFTEEN

Deceitful Proceedings

I awoke at 5.55am on 10 May 2002, five minutes before Vasoon the guard changed duties. He wished me well and said he would pray for a good result. I knew he was genuine as throughout my stay he was more than considerate and gave me a very small bible as a present, which was unfortunately lost in the hospital.

Following breakfast, I showered and dressed and packed my belongings. Although my emergency passport was already prepared along with airline tickets and other documents, I was unknowingly and officially not discharged from the hospital. At 8am, Alpheus Sibila came alone and argued with hospital staff over something that was unknown to me. The heightened tension and his aggressive behaviour unnerved me. We walked to the prison van waiting in a side entrance to the hospital and drove the short journey to Chatsworth Police Station where it was necessary for him to complete paperwork. As we prepared to go to court, he once again smirked, "Your fancy lawyer will get you nowhere."

To consume oneself with unnecessary fears when one knows that those fears are reality, is futile. Instead, I thought about the magistrate who was a cartoonist's dream and resembled a female version of Fred Flintstone, only with a vicious devious streak. She had short legs, a stumpy nose and even walked like the character. In reality she was anything but funny and possessed an ominous cynicism, although she appeared extremely nervous as if she lacked the courage of her convictions. I thought her personality was overtly subdued at times and she expressed traits of homophobia, which would be indicative of her faith. A complicated questionable character altogether.

The prosecutor on the other hand, lacked professional panache with an undignified approach to her profession and would have been more suited to a circus than a court of law. She resembled the Wicked Witch of the West, but this miniature woman was beyond the realms of doubt a caricature. Had I been a talented cartoonist, I could have drawn Fred Flintstone sitting on a bench with a wicked witch trying desperately to close the box they had opened, but alas it was far too late. Pandora's Box was well and truly opened and the duo would later be castigated by their peers for their performance.

The wagon slowed up as we descended into the underground of the court complex. The arrogant Alpheus Sibila ordered me out of the wagon and I was led into a small holding cell where two other black men were awaiting a court appearance. One had been in Westville for thirty months for rape and murder and was pleading innocent at a remand hearing. I was flabbergasted at his casual approach to his fate.

I was then taken upstairs to an outer office belonging to the State Prosecutor, which had been commandeered by my advocate Mr Howse, so that he could advise me on the way the trial would go. I gave serious thought to the plea, but with the powerful threat of the Mansoors hanging over me and with the knowledge I possessed, I knew they would carry out their actions without due thought or consideration.

Although I said I would not consume myself with fear, I was going against my own judgment and drifting in that direction. It appeared that I would be deported and although innocent of the charges except for count one by association with regard to my visa for remaining in the country, I was going to plead guilty. The prosecutor repeatedly entered the room, interrupting our meeting to use the telephone. I watched this tiny bulge with the laugh of a hyena, acting like a schoolgirl, mocking the advocate behind his back and whispering unkind words to friends about me. Jimmy Howse was far more superior and professional than the iniquitous State Prosecutor.

The plea of guilty meant that the case would be heard forthwith and it appeared that the sentence would be a fine and deportation, or perhaps a fine and a warning. A prison sentence was unthinkable. A plea of "not guilty" would mean awaiting trial for possibly up to two years or more in prison and it was highly unlikely that I would be granted bail and a visa prior to the trial, as I would be considered a flight risk. I had been sedated prior to departure from the hospital and I was also in a confused state of mind, but I feared their threats, as now I was acutely aware they were dangerous, ruthless people. I was given a copy of my charge sheet 41/928/02 as we left the prosecutor's den for the courtroom.

Members of the public had gathered along with my family, who looked tense as they awaited the magistrate's entry. Following the opening formalities, I was called to the stand where I could see the judge swaying in front of me. I tried desperately to concentrate as I stood in the dock, but although I had been given medication in the hospital, my back pain worsened. I even considered asking if I could sit down, but refrained from doing so for fear of yet another refusal, as with the many glasses of water that I had been denied in the past. I gave my full name and the questioning commenced.

Mr Howse asked me if it was true that I was Irish and that I had lived most of my life in Ireland. I replied that he was correct in his assumption.

"Mr Ledwidge, is it true that you are gay?"

The eyes of the court looked directly at me as I replied, "That is correct."

The prosecutor wrote with speed as the questioning continued.

"And I think there will be no complaints if I lead you on this," said Howse, "Is it further correct that you are an openly gay person and have spoken in public and in the media, including radio and television on the subject?"

"That is correct."

"Ireland is a Catholic stronghold, is it?" he asked.

"That is correct."

"And what is the attitude towards the gay community there?"

"There is very little change although following the directive of legislation from the European Parliament, they are more understanding at times."

"Mr Ledwidge, have you ever had any works relating to the gay community published?"

"Yes I have."

"What is that?"

"*To Live the Impossible Dream.*"

"And have they been sold publicly?"

"They have, yes."

"I'd like you to tell Her Worship what links there have been with the former Prime Minister of Ireland, Mary Robinson?"

I interrupted him, "I beg to differ on that one, she was the President of Ireland."

"The President, I beg your pardon."

"Mary Robinson was President of Ireland, Your Worship, for seven years. She is a barrister or advocate by profession, and in that role and prior to her accession as President, she led the campaign in the courts in the 1980s on behalf of one David Norris, in order to have the 1861 British law on the Irish statue books concerning the Offences Against the Person Act dealing with homosexuality changed. The case was lost in Ireland, but won in the Court of Human Rights in Europe, prompting the Irish Government to rectify the law, which they did. Following her term as President, she became the United Nations High Commissioner for Human Rights."

"Which position she currently holds?" asked the advocate.

"The book was dedicated to Mary Robinson, in appreciation for what she did."

"I see. I recall she featured prominently a year or so ago in the Conference against Racism, the World Conference, here in Durban."

"Yes."

"Were you here, or were you in any way involved?"

"Yes, I was here. I was not at the International Conference Centre, but I did deliver a speech in a venue around the corner from it."

The advocate went on to note the various charities I had been involved with over many years relating to the

AIDS crisis, including an orphanage with young disabled people in Umlazi, South Africa. He went on to ask about my family ties with the South African people, saying that two of my sisters were married to South Africans. He pointed out the number of visits I had made to the country, along with friends and family, in order to paint a picture for the court that I was not one of your uncouth aliens. Then he produced the Irish Police Clearance Certificate and a personal letter from a high-ranking officer regarding my honourable character.

He said, "This proves that the accused was doing everything by the book and clarifies his age and date of birth." These were handed up as exhibits. The judge showed no emotion whilst the prosecutor wrote steadfastly, always with a permanent grin on her face.

"Now, there is some correspondence that I have been given by my instructing attorney, indicating that time appeared to be of the essence in the Casa Blanc [*the guest house I was purchasing*] deal. I am going to hand this letter to you. It is from HBZ Insurance brokers. It is from Khan, Habib Khan, and indicates, 'Please be advised we are in the process of obtaining a bond for Mr Ledwidge. We will also be pleased if you would grant an extension of at least another month until 20 November, as we are awaiting documents from Home Affairs.' Do you confirm that?" he asked politely.

"Yes I do."

"Do I understand that the delay in getting your necessary paperwork through Home Affairs was a concern insofar as the purchase of the property was concerned?"

"Yes that is correct."

"Just explain that to us?"

"Well when Habib Khan had promised the seller of the property, Mrs Patricia Lerm, that the deal would be settled in early November, Mrs Lerm became very impatient because she wanted the deal settled as quickly as possible. Khan was stringing her along, offering all kinds of excuses and delaying tactics and so on. He had all of my documentation and there was little I could do about it."

"Okay, right, then there is the matter of the Casa Blanc letterhead signed 'Patricia' and I'll just read the contents to you and if the prosecutor has no objection, I'd ask to hand this one in. It reads, 'Dear Joupee', I understand that this is Joupee Joubert that we… that would be the Cape Town representative of Acutts Real Estate, Joubert is it?"

"Peter Joubert."

"Yes, 'Re: Home Affairs. Thank you for your letter from Mr Khan forwarded to me.' That would be Habib Khan, would it?"

"Yes."

"'I agree herewith to extend the date to 20 November, Could you please contact Liam and inform, in the event of him trying to speed up his application with Home Affairs, I might also be able to find out the status of his application. In order to do so, I need the following'… and she gives details of what she needs. 'I am hoping to have all matters finalised before December 2001 as I would like to plan ahead.'"

"Yes."

"Do you confirm this?"

"Yes."

"I see that it was also faxed to you," he stated curiously.

"Yes."

"Mr Ledwidge, does that give the background as to why your application was so urgent?"

"Yes."

"Okay, alright, you've indicated in your plea you weren't aware of what Habib Khan was up to until you saw the false marriage certificate."

"That is correct."

"Just explain to Her Worship what your mandate was to Khan."

"Well I have never known anything to be so confused. I went to Acutts Real Estate, as I was interested in buying property in Cape Town. They introduced me to one of their alleged freelance agents, namely Habib Khan, and as their representative he was to look after the bond and the process of permanent residency. He came to our home in Mobeni where I filled out an immigration questionnaire. I gave him my medical records as requested for Home Affairs. I also gave him my passport, police clearance, tax clearance and 47,000 rands [£4,700] for what he claimed were bank charges and administration fees."

"Did you understand at this stage that the documentation was going to be acquired lawfully?"

"Yes, naturally I did."

"And also in your plea you indicated that when he came with the false marriage certificate, you realised that things were not being done lawfully by acquiescing in whatever he and others then did?"

"Yes."

"Okay, I would like to deal with the aspects of funds that you brought into the country. Can you indicate to

Her Worship how much you brought into South Africa during the period of your stay?"

"Approximately 830,000 [£83,000] and 1,000,000 rands, [£100,000]."

"Okay, I have a copy of your bank statement. Can you confirm that this reflects the deposits and withdrawals during that period, basically the period November through to January?"

"Yes."

"Have you had sight of this?"

"I have seen it, yes."

"And just to give Her Worship a breakdown of the more significant withdrawal, or the most significant withdrawal of 600,000 rands [£60,000]."

"That is correct."

"Can you indicate to the court who that was paid to?"

"Ahmed Yacoob Mansoor."

"Are they the Mansoor family mentioned in your plea?"

"That is correct."

"What was that payment for?"

"It was in relation to the bond, as I was led to believe that 200,000 rands, [£20,000] was a deposit, 12,500 rands, [£1250] was legal fees and the balance of 387,500 rands, [£38,750] for VAT and transfer fees."

"Alright then, what have you now discovered?"

"Well, the whole deal has gone sour."

"The bottom line is that there is a disagreement of fact between the Mansoors as to what the money was for and this is now a civil action."

"That's right."

"I see. Are the Mansoors still in possession of the 600,000 rands [£60,000]?"

"I have no idea."

"As far as you know?"

"Yes."

"Okay, did the Mansoors seek other monies from you?"

"Yes."

"How much was that?"

"There was a grand piano at Casa Blanc which was a feature in the reception area and Ahmed Mansoor said that the proprietor Patricia Lerm was in need of money and if I bought the piano for 80,000 rands [£8,000] she would speed up the negotiations and allow us in on occupational rent. He asked me to release 60,000 rands, [£6,000] which I did, and several weeks later he said, 'She is now prepared to let you in if you pay the balance of 20,000 rands [£2,000].' I met with Mrs Lerm on the Waterfront in Cape Town and gave her the 20,000 rands, [£2,000] being the balance of the 80,000 rands, [£8,000]. She was shocked as she had sold the piano for 40,000 rands, [£4,000] and not the 80,000 rands, [£8,000], as described by Ahmed Mansoor. He pocketed the 40,000 rands [£4,000]."

"Now Mr Ledwidge, I've also been given a letter that was addressed to you by Mr Ahmed Mansoor and it is claiming over and above the 600,000 rands, [£60,000]. It is fees, (this was Mansoor trying to make up costs in the event of litigation against him, as these costs were already paid as calculated by the solicitor Zayed Paruk, of Lockhat & Associates), 151,000 rands, [£15,100] and some odd rands for Ahmed's disbursements and an amount of 400,000 rands, [£40,000] for, what he terms as, Sadek's disposal in terms of a second mandate. Now do you confirm that those monies were also demanded of you?"

"Yes I do."

The eminent advocate looked at the magistrate and cast a keen eye on the State Prosecutor, who nervously pulled on her tunic and said, "Now then, it's the next paragraph that follows that I am most interested and concerned about and which has bearing on this matter. Again, with the permission of the prosecutor, I am going to hand this one up. Firstly, do you agree that you received this letter?"

"Yes."

"Okay, I'd just like to read the first paragraph, and it says 'Should you not respond timeously [and that means to those demands for those monies] I, and on behalf of Sadek, through Attorneys Lockhart And Associates, will be launching in Durban High Court an application with costs to obtain such relief that I may be entitled to in law. I will be citing the following parties, against who I will be seeking no relief.

a. The department of Home Affairs to establish whether you are an alien.
b. Your Spouse to establish your Marriage Contract as she may be responsible for your debts incurred.
c. The South African police/Interpol to establish whether you are wanted for any criminal investigation.'

Do you confirm that these threats were issued?"

"Yes, I do."

"Alright, so that we can deal with them one by one, did the Mansoors know that the documentation was false, in other words, the subject matter of the charges?"

"Yes they did."

"And the Ismail Mansoor was, in fact, one of the Mansoors which you refer to here?"

"That is correct."

"He is the person who corrupted one of the Home Affairs Officials?"

"I guess so."

"Does it follow, that therefore, when they were saying 'to establish whether you were an alien' they very well knew that you were an alien, but just wanted to report to the authorities in order to extort from you?"

"That is correct."

"Okay, and then, 'Your Spouse, to establish your marriage contract', did they know that you were not married?"

"They did, yes."

"And Muniaama Moodley?"

"Yes, they knew."

"And again, did you interpret this as a threat to expose?"

"Yes, I did."

"How did you respond to those demands?"

"I didn't."

"What happened next?"

"When I came back from Cape Town, I made an appointment with the Mansoors to get my money back. I arranged to meet them on Monday 22 April at 8pm, but when I arrived, he said the money was not possible until the next day and that I should return there at 12 noon. I explained that we had a family funeral to attend and so he should suggest another day. We agreed on Wednesday 24 April at 12 noon, but in the meantime as we were preparing for the funeral the next morning, the two officials from the department of Home Affairs came and arrested me at home."

"Do you know who reported you to the officials?"

"I do not."

"Do you have any idea?"

"Yes."

"Who is that?"

The prosecutor looked directly at me as I stared back and said, "Ahmed Yacoob Mansoor."

"Right, I'd just like to deal briefly with your profile in this country. I'd like to refer to an original of a newspaper report in 2001. Do I understand this was a previous visit?"

"That is correct."

"Obviously I don't want to read the whole article, but perhaps you can indicate to Her Worship what this was all about when you took exception to the comment of a certain public official."

"I had criticised the Lord Mayor over his remarks against the gay community and reminded him that as first citizen he represented all the people of Durban. He apologised. I was talking about freedom and freedom rights and how South Africa had come a long way since the apartheid years. I was talking about the oppression of freedom. The press happened to pick up on my remarks regarding the Mayor."

"Right, it also states here publicly that you intended coming to live in South Africa?"

"That is correct."

"Mr Ledwidge, I have to ask you, were you planning anything illegal in this country?"

"Certainly not."

"It is also a concern for the court to know how this all affects the country's economy. Could you just explain whether what's happened in this case had any adverse effect on the country's economy, or the potential for adverse effect?"

"Well, I believe South Africa as a new developing nation needs foreign investors. My investment was comparatively small, but it is from small acorns that mighty trees are grown. I personally found throughout my many trips here that this country has great scope for development and I felt that the people would be happy to see foreign investors. It is with regret, however, that following my own personal experiences here in your country that the aforementioned is not the case and would without doubt turn people away from investing in this country, where it appears you can trust no one."

"Alright, now there is one concern of course, and that is the lady Muniaama Moodley. You realise now of course one of the implications of what happened is that, as far as the official records are concerned, you and she are married."

"Yes."

"And of course, that does carry some implications or some potential implications. You realise that?"

"Yes."

"Is there anything you would like to say to the court or to the person Muniaama Moodley – I understand she is here – in this regard?"

"Well, first and foremost, I would like to apologise to Mrs Moodley for what has happened to her. I was completely unaware, as she was, about any marriage and I simply knew nothing about his intentions. I didn't know anything about a marriage and I have never met

Mrs Moodley. I don't even know what she looks like other than what I saw on the marriage certificate and for what has occurred, I apologise profusely to her."

"Your future plans as to where you will live, Mr Ledwidge?"

"Back in Ireland."

"You're going? You agree that you're not going to fight any deportation order?"

"No."

"You will immediately return to Ireland?"

"That is correct."

"You agree to pay any necessary costs of deportation with the Aliens Act?"

"Yes, I do."

"And you are available to return to Ireland immediately?"

"Yes, I am."

"Right, now the prosecution has indicated, and I'm not quite sure why, but they have indicated that they might be suggesting that a jail term is appropriate in the circumstances for you, and on this score I'd like us to concentrate on your health. What is the current state of your health?"

"Well these and recent events have traumatised me greatly. I have never been in jail before and I have never been in trouble with the law. It has not only traumatised me, it has traumatised my family. My mother left here the other day and she will be 70 at the end of the month, along with her 78-year-old friend. It has upset the whole family, here and in Ireland, the UK, Canada and the United States."

"Right, Dr Kanjee did put on record how your period in detention, awaiting the outcome of these proceedings, has affected your health. Can you possibly tell us a little more? I understand that you have been seen by a psychiatrist?"

"Yes."

"What was that in connection with?"

"Well, she wanted to know the full story, which I gave her. She asked me if I was suicidal, I said I was. I told her my faith in humanity had dropped to zero as there appeared to be so much dishonesty and corruption in your country. I cannot eat properly, I cannot sleep properly and I was simply in a traumatic state over the whole affair."

"Thank you. Your Worship, I have nothing further."

SIXTEEN

Naked Corruption

It was the turn of the prosecutor to interrogate as she dragged herself to her feet, constantly smirking and looking at the spectators as opposed to facing the court.

"Do you accept that Ahmed Yacoob Mansoor actually sought an interdict at the High Court restraining you from directly or indirectly assaulting, verbally, abusing, threatening or intimidating him?"

"I never assaulted, I never threatened him and I never received *that* by the way," I retorted.

"Sorry?" she asked.

"I never received that document."

"You never received the interdict?"

"No, I did not."

"Okay."

"You see, I was never given it to respond to."

"You see this was also… let me show it to you. This interdict was against your brother-in-law, Dr Kanjee, as well as Sean Govender. Do you want to have a look at it?"

"Yes. Nobody harassed or threatened the Mansoors. Has it not entered your head that under such circumstances they should have called the police? Instead they run to their corrupt friends in high places to issue such nonsense. Their facts are erroneous."

She retorted and bellowed like an actress at the Old Vic, "Do you agree that there was an interdict sought against you?"

"Well, I've seen it now for what it's worth."

"Now Sir, with regard to the 600,000 rands [£60,000], have you issued any civil proceedings against the Mansoors for this money?"

"No, I have not."

"Why not?"

"I have been biding my time, hoping that the matter would be resolved peacefully."

In an amazing twist, they tried to involve Patricia Lerm the owner of Casa Blanc, the Cape Town property I was purchasing, when she asked me a question that, firstly took me by surprise and, secondly, I really did not understand.

"You are aware that the State is investigating the question of fraud in respect of this agreement with Vulship and Patricia Lerm?"

"No, I was not aware of that. How could there—"

She cut me short.

"You were in court on Wednesday when the State made an application for the matter to be postponed?"

"Was that in the morning?"

There were whispers and then she re-thought her strategy.

"Who is the proprietor/director of Vulship?"

"Ahmed Yacoob Mansoor."

The blood drained from her face as she looked at her notes as she didn't realise that he owned the company. After a brief moment she composed herself.

"Why did you get involved with the Mansoors? Why did you not get your brother-in-law Dr Kanjee, or your other brother-in-law, who is also South African?"

"Well, he resides outside the state. My brother-in-law here is far too busy and the Mansoors were trusted, loyal family friends of ours and it was they themselves who suggested that they come on board."

"Now, with regard to your apology to Mrs Moodley, the widow whose name was used and you allegedly married, why did you find it necessary to perpetuate this fraud when you found out about it?"

"Because I did not know what to do about it and it was the Mansoors who said they would have the matter resolved themselves."

"Did you not consider the person's feelings at that stage and how it would affect her?"

"I was informed she knew nothing about it. It was a matter of administration and it would be rectified."

"Okay, when she knew about it, did you not think about that?"

"I was incarcerated."

"While you were incarcerated, did you not think about that?"

"I did, but there was little I could do and I was told to leave it to my lawyers."

"So you didn't even think about her feelings?"

"Of course I did."

"And how do you think this woman feels, being married to somebody she doesn't even know and being a widow."

"I understand, but I have only been informed of the full facts recently."

"Okay, now you have said that you have been traumatised through this whole ordeal?"

"Yes."

"The State is going to lead evidence of Mrs Moodley to show how traumatised she was when she found out about this."

"Yes, I understand."

"Now, do you think that your traumatic experience is worse than hers?"

"I've no idea."

"And why do you think the State should consider your traumatic feelings above hers and give you a lenient sentence?"

"We are both victims of circumstance entirely not of our own doing. It's a matter for the Court."

"Thank you, no further questions, Your Worship."

I was then told to leave the witness box.

My advocate then advised the Court that I had completed my evidence, at which point the prosecutor called my alleged wife Muniaama Moodley. The Magistrate showed her compassion and offered her a seat in the witness box, as the State Prosecutor proceeded to ask her some questions.

"Ma'am, could you tell the Court how old you are?"

"I am 49."

"And is it correct that you are a widow?"

"Yes."

"When did your husband pass away?"

"In 1982."

"'82. How many children do you have Ma'am?"

"Four."

"Is it correct that they are all four daughters?"

"Yes."

"And how old are they?"

"26, 24, 23, 16."

"And is it correct, Ma'am, that on 25 April you were approached by two immigration officials who informed you that you were allegedly married to Mr Ledwidge?"

"Yes."

"Did you know anything about this marriage?"

"No."

"Could you tell the Court what happened to you when you found out about it?"

"I was shocked, sick. I got headache."

"Sorry?"

"I was shocked."

"And how did this affect your health Ma'am?"

"From that day up to today I have been very sick. When I get shocked, I suffer with runny tummy and headache and stress."

"And have you sought medical attention for your illness since then?"

"Yes."

"How many times have you been to the doctor since then?"

"Twice."

"For treatment for your sickness?"

"Yes."

"And how has it affected your daughters, Ma'am?"

"They are very upset and it was very traumatising as well as my family as well. They are shocked and they feel it is not right. You know it's embarrassing."

"Okay, now, it is correct that you are a Tamil widow and this has religious connotations to you?"

"Yes it does, it does."

She then proceeded to lead the witness, "Could you tell the Court how this affected you? In fact, once you're a Tamil and you lose your dot and thali, you don't put it on again. You don't ever get married again and the fact that Mr Ledwidge is a white male, a foreigner… how did this affect your family and yourself?"

"They did get upset because he is from a different race and I am a different race," she replied.

"And also you questioned if this was true?"

"Yes."

"And in fact this led for an embarrassment for you?"

"Yes, yes," she replied excitedly in agreement, much to the satisfaction of the prosecutor."

"Did you have any intention of marrying after your husband died?"

"No."

"And do you understand that you have to make statements and attend the Home Affairs to actually get this marriage annulled?"

"Yes."

"And actually to ensure that some sort of annulment… ensure that the papers are sorted out and that you're reverted back to your status of being a widow?"

"Yes."

There was an interruption from my advocate Jimmy Howes.

"Your Worship, if I could change that word, 'that you have to…'"

The Magistrate, clearly annoyed at the interruption, looked at the State Prosecutor and ordered sternly, "Miss Prosecutor change the wording."

The prosecutor continued. "That you have to attend Home Affairs and ensure that all paperwork is sorted out so that you are reverted back to the status of being a widow."

"Yes."

"Now the defence has handed up a letter to the Court (Ahmed Mansoor), which indicates that certain creditors or would-be creditors of the accused can also seek action-relief from you for his debts. They actually indicate that they will look at the spouse for payments of debts." *(These were trumped-up debts of Ahmed Mansoor who fraudulently sought money from me. Monies he actually owed me, I had no debts whatsoever.)*

Mrs Moodley became hysterical in the witness box. "No, no but I've got nothing," at which point Mr Howse intervened.

"No Your Worship, that's completely and utterly misleading the witness. We handed that up simply to show that—"

The magistrate intervened, "Well, I understand that spouse would mean the accused's normal spouse, not the—"

The prosecutor jumped to her feet, "The accused is not married, Your Worship. This is the only spouse."

The argument heated up as an agitated Mr Howse said, "No, no he is not married. Your Worship, so they were meaning this—"

The magistrate interrupted yet again, "So they were meaning this lady?"

Mr Howse addressed the magistrate, "They were indeed. But, Your Worship, it was indicated that they were doing so in full knowledge that she is not his spouse and it was purely extortive in nature. In other words, all they were seeking to do was to use that as a threat to expose the fraud. Not that they ever contemplated suing the lady before you."

The magistrate, clearly on the side of the Mansoors, said, "Well Mr Howse that is a matter for argument."

Mr Howse looked at her and said, "Well that was the—"

She interrupted him again and said in a callous tone, "The witness would never know the difference."

He continued, "I'm just pointing out what the evidence was, Your Worship. There was no threat whatsoever that she would be sued by those people. That's been the evidence."

The prosecutor was determined and quoted again from the letter, but after causing a commotion and frightening the witness, she stopped and nearly choked on her words when she read, "Against whom I will be seeking no relief."

"No relief," said the advocate.

The prosecutor apologised and continued, repeating herself in a perceptibly uptight manner, "Now Ma'am, how has this whole episode made you feel?"

Once more Mrs Moodley told her how sick she had felt and then the prosecutor asked, "Are you scared, Ma'am?"

"Yes. Because I am not used to going to court and, you know, that I am always at home and to me this is all, is like a shock to me."

"Okay. No further questions. Your Worship."

Jimmy Howse, in his professional wisdom, was to unearth the true feelings of this witness and expose the Court and the State for misleading and exaggerating the circumstances. It was a masterly performance and an education in law itself. He stood and looked compassionately at the diminutive Tamil widow and said softly, "Mrs Moodley, you said you are not used to coming to court and it's shocking for you. Who wanted you to come to court?"

She became inaudible, so he then asked her, "Is it correct to say that the prosecutor and the immigration officials wanted you in court?"

"Yes."

"That's right, Mrs Moodley. Have you still got your identity document with you? I see you are holding it in your hand there, Mrs Moodley, yes? Does your identity document show that you are married to your husband and that you are now widowed?"

"Yes."

"No, this is a new identity book," he stated, as she burst out, "Yes, yes!"

"What does it show for your marriage details? Could I have a look? May I approach, Your Worship?"

Mr Howse looked at the document and replied, "Oh, I see this is a new one. It's got no record of any marriage or anything in it."

"No," she replied apprehensively.

"Okay, so you agree, Mrs Moodley, that it's not shown in your identity book that you are married to anyone else?"

"Yes," she said sheepishly.

"So please tell Her Worship… sorry, what is your standard of education?"

"I left school in Standard 7."

"Standard 7, okay. Are you working?"

"No."

"Okay, I would like you to tell Her Worship, why did you see this as bad? What do you understand about why it's bad and why are you upset about what happened and when you discovered that the records indicate that you are not married to Mr Ledwidge?"

There was suppressed laughter when she turned to the magistrate and said, "Your Honour, can I ask my daughter to take the stand?"

The magistrate looked down sternly at her and said, "You have to answer the question Mrs Moodley. Just tell us why you feel so bad about it."

Clearly frustrated, she replied, "Because all of a sudden on the 25th, somebody comes and tells you you're married and you don't know this person and you haven't met this person."

Mr Howse calmed her and said, "Ya, we hear you. We hear you on that Mrs Moodley, on that."

He then asked gently, "But explain to us why it is so bad in your understanding? We'd just like to hear from you, why you feel it is so bad?"

"It is bad that you don't know this person and they say you are married, it's shocking. All of a sudden somebody comes to your door and says you are a married person."

"Alright. So it's nothing more than that, Mrs Moodley, is it only that?"

"Ya," she replied.

"That somebody came to your door and said that you are married?

"Yes."

"Do you understand that according to the law, in actual fact you were never married to Mr Ledwidge? Do you understand that?"

"No," she murmured.

"But do you understand that your identity book shows that you were never married to this man?"

There was a pause for thought and she said, "Ya."

"You understand that okay, so the only thing is that you feel bad because somebody came and told you?"

"Yes."

"Alright, and then you said also because of your religion and you say he is a white man?"

"Yes."

"And you say it's an embarrassment to you?"

"Yes."

"Now, Mrs Moodley, Mr Ledwidge has apologised. He has explained to the court that he did not arrange the marriage certificate. It was done by a Mr Khan and he has apologised. Do you accept his apology?"

There was complete silence in the court as all eyes, including those of the magistrate and prosecutor were fixed on Moodley. There was no reply as Mr Howse pursued an answer.

"Are you prepared to accept his apology when he says that he is sorry for the fact that you got shocked when you were told?"

"Yes. Another thing, what he put me through is… it's very traumatising."

"Yes, but I am telling you now that he is saying that he is sorry for any trauma that you have undergone. Do you accept his apology?"

She finally relented and said, "Yes."

The advocate leaned forward and gently put his last question to her, "And Mrs Moodley, he says that he now wants to go back to Ireland, to his country. Do you accept that?" She looked bemused and uttered, "That I wouldn't know. The Court has to decide."

"Okay, so you leave it in the hands of the Court?"

She was barely audible as she uttered, "Yes."

"Alright, thank you. Thank you, Your Worship."

She sat looking straight ahead as the magistrate said "Mrs Moodley, you said that in the Tamil culture you're supposed to not wear your dot and thali anymore?"

"Yes."

"So you are a staunch Tamil?"

"Yes."

"And you attend the services… the temple regularly?"

"Yes, I go to the one in 706."

"Are you a staunch member of the Tamil community?"

"Yes, Ma'am"

"Do you perform the entire religious rites etcetera that is wanted of you as a Tamil?"

"Yes, Your Honour."

I remember asking myself, why all the fuss, and whether Mrs Moodley really was a staunch Tamil. How did one explain a daughter of sixteen when her husband had died twenty years previously? I was apologising to this innocent woman who had become the victim of Habib Khan and because my name was used by him, I felt obligated to her as any normal person would feel. In an ironic way, we had both become victims of this predator who preyed on foreigners to extort money. The magistrate looked pitifully down on her and said, "Thank you, you may stand down."

I stared at Mrs Moodley as she walked past me, but her eyes never met mine. I genuinely felt sorry that a man like Khan had used her for his own personal gain and the

Mansoors had used her to maximise their strength of the case by playing on the woman's emotions and vulnerability.

SEVENTEEN

Perpetuating the Corruption

The State Prosecutor proceeded to call Vala Prabashan Naidoo and opened her line of questioning by saying, "Sir, is it correct that you're a Chief Immigration Officer stationed at Durban International Airport?"

"That is so."

"And that you have held that post for the past five years?"

"That is so."

"Is it correct that you are overseeing the entire investigation with regard to Home Affairs and the fraud perpetuated against Home Affairs against Liam Ledwidge?"

"That is correct."

"Now, in this case, the accused has been convicted of contravening one count of the Aliens Control Act, actually remaining in the country when his permit had expired and then seeking to obtain permanent residence by virtue of the marriage. How common is this sort of offence, Sir?"

"Ma'am, we have found since '99 after the Constitutional Court ruling, Dawood and Others versus The Minister of Home Affairs, that the incidents and influx of foreign nationals coming into the country to obtain fraudulent documentation to acquire permanent residence has escalated quite dramatically. We are inundated with such cases and it is a problem."

"Approximate amount of cases?"

"Ma'am, I will say since 1999, there have been literally hundreds of these cases throughout the country."

"What about the problem at Home Affairs with regard to corruption? How rife is that?"

"It is increasingly becoming a problem. There have been a number of Home Affairs' officials recently in our Durban, Umgeni Road Office that have been detained on charges of corruption. In fact, last Friday there was an official detained on allegations of issuing false certificates… marriage certificates."

"So, in fact, is there some sort of syndicate operating within Home Affairs and outside?"

"We seem to think so Ma'am."

"What are some of the problems, other problems experienced with aliens in the country?"

"I'll try to be brief. It is quite a long story to get into, but you normally find that illegal immigrants cause a lot of problems to South Africa as a whole. One of the main reasons for them coming into the country is to acquire work in many cases. They obviously take up works that South Africans would have got. In many cases, they are paid poorly. By taking up this work, they create unemployment for the South African citizen. This, of course, you know, leads to a whole lot of socio-economic problems. But, more importantly, what disturbs us a lot is the criminal aspect that we have come across recently. I mean, one is also familiar with the drug syndicates, car theft syndicates and prostitution rings that are generally run by some of these foreign nationals. There's been also often in the news and in the papers and, ja, it does pose a big problem for us. More recently we have noticed that there is an increase in conmen and fraudsters coming into the country and praying on innocent citizens as well for their own purpose."

"How many illegal aliens are there in South Africa?"

"How many are there? A conservative estimate Ma'am in excess of five million."

"Was that the recent figure quoted in the newspaper?"

"That's correct."

"Thank you Sir, no further questions."

The magistrate invited Advocate Howse to cross-examine the witness.

"Mr Naidoo, you will agree that the typical alien against whom the legislation is aimed is the person you've described. He is normally a person who is either a refugee from his own country, or he's not quite making it in that country and he is coming here seeking employment, or seeking to do some illegal activity in circumstances where he knows that this country won't accept him if he applies for citizenship."

"That is correct."

"So you go along, that is basically the definition of your average alien?"

"I'd use the word average, yes."

"Okay. In the case of the accused before the Court do you know of any reason why, if he had made proper application for temporary residence, why he would not have been successful?"

He began to fidget and became nervous before replying.

"I don't really understand your question, Sir."

"Alright. Let me rephrase it. If the accused before the Court made a proper formal application for temporary residence and later for permanent residence, do you know of any reason why it would not have been successful?"

"Well, firstly, Sir, he made the application under the wrong category. There are various categories and clearly this category that he chose—"

At that moment the magistrate intervened and said, "No, I don't think you understand the question."

Mr Howse informed him, "No you are misunderstanding me."

He blushed and coughed before replying, "I am sorry, I am not really with you."

The perturbed magistrate said, "Try again Mr Howse, just rephrase."

"Yes, you are misunderstanding me completely. The accused – it's on record – always wanted to come to South Africa, alright. He got all of his clearance papers from Ireland. We've handed up Exhibits B and C, two documents showing that he is a person of good standing in Ireland. No criminal record. He's got a character reference that was going to be used as the basis for application, alright. He came over here with an excess of one million rands, a lot of money, which he was going to invest in the country. Now, with that as the basis for his application, if he had filled in all forms correctly, Mr Naidoo, and he'd made a substantive application to the authorities to allow him to stay here lawfully, do you know of any reason why that would not have been successful?"

"Oh, I see what you mean. I can give my opinion, but as you know, there is a Special Immigration Selection Committee that actually sits and hears these applications."

"Yes, so I suppose if all the criteria were met, then obviously there wouldn't have been any problems with him obtaining that?"

"Sure, yes, I am inclined to agree with you," said a nervous Naidoo, looking down at Sibila and Bigela.

"That sort of applicant like Mr Ledwidge here, a man of good standing, of good background, of some wealth, who will be able to be an asset to the country and to the economy will usually be successful in his application if he makes it properly. You agree with that?"

"Ja, I would assume so."

"Okay. So straight away there, he is much different to, for example, the Nigerians who are coming in with no work, no money and they just want to conduct a drug syndicate or, as you say, the conmen are now rife and the motor vehicle thieves and so on. You agree they are much different to him?"

"It's hard for me to really comment Sir with any real clarity, because I don't know the character of Mr Ledwidge that well."

The advocate looked sternly at him, as if to wonder what kind of intellect he was dealing with and so he continued. "Okay. I don't know his background as you know. There are certain allegations that are still being investigated. So it's difficult for me to make an informed choice to the questions you're asking me."

"Alright. But do you know of any allegations that there are in existence in relation to the purchase of a house or his guest house to run it as a business?"

"That's what I've been hearing, yes."

"Yes. Okay. Alright. How long does an application take, Mr Naidoo, a formal proper substantive application, for temporary residence and then permanent residence?"

"Okay, the procedure is such that you first obtain a marriage certificate and apply for a temporary residence permit."

At this point Mr Howse was aware that Naidoo was stringing him along, by pretending not to understand and misdirecting his answers in an attempt to avoid the fundamental questions.

"No, no, no, let's say somebody who is not married. Let's say Mr Ledwidge now, he is applying, he is unmarried. He is making a substantive application. He is filling in all the forms and so on. How long does the whole process take before he will eventually be given permanent residency?"

"They normally take up to a year for the actual applications to be processed and for the committee to sit and make a final decision."

"So you agree it's a long process?"

"No, definitely."

"And the name Habib Khan, that's familiar to you isn't it?"

"Well I've heard it since the case came up."

"Okay. But you saw that his picture is with the authorities and he is being sought?"

"That is correct."

"For contraventions of this kind?"

"That is correct."

"That's right. Now, I'm going to put to you that what happened here was that Habib Khan was breaking the deal for the accused to purchase that property in Cape Town to run it as a guest house. The seller of the property was impatient. She wanted the deal to go through within a month. Khan was given the mandate to do all the things necessary to arrange the temporary and permanent residency, so that he could purchase the house, and because time was of the essence and Khan with all his contacts, as we know, decided to take the illegal route. Now you can't dispute that. That's actually in the plea."

"Well I accept that."

"Yes, okay. And then as far as your department is concerned, I understand one of your priorities, when a case of this sort is finalised, is to deport the person."

"Yes."

At this point the magistrate ordered a break for lunch and I was taken to the cells below the court, which were full to capacity with black prisoners. When I entered there was an unnerving silence. I was locked in and this was an unsettling experience, but within minutes, a guard arrived and ordered me out for my own safety. I was escorted to an adjoining cell with two rough-edged blacks awaiting a date for their trial for multiple murders. They eyed me up and down in an unsettling manner, but when I offered them a cigarette each, the atmosphere changed slightly, although their gorilla-like features scared me to bits. I asked for some water, but I was refused. I never received lunch.

We were back in court with Prabashan Naidoo still under oath.

My advocate continued with his line of questioning, "Mr Naidoo, what is the usual procedure adopted by your department in cases of this sort? Is it not that in many cases, you actually follow the administrative route where you take the person into custody yourself and you use the procedures described in the Act, whereby you then repatriate the person without charging them in court?"

"To be honest with you, Sir, prior to '99 we found that these cases were few and far between and instead of going through a lengthy court procedure and having a lengthy term of imprisonment for the accused at great expense to the State, it was decided at that stage that it was easier to simply ask the accused to give them a fine, an admission of guilt fine, and then to repatriate the accused at his own expense. But since then things have changed drastically, as I stated earlier, with the influx of these cases and, of course, the department is now seeking to have these sentences passed that will serve as a deterrence for such abuses to stop in the future. So the penalties that we hope the Courts will impose in the future will be much stricter than what happened in the past."

Mr Howse continued, "I want you to answer me honestly. Is it not correct that today, these days, you still use that administrative procedure? You don't bring every case to court?"

"Well that is left entirely up to the senior person in charge of the immigration section."

"I know, I know, Inspector... oh sorry, Chief Inspector. But I want you to answer my question. Isn't it in reality the case that several matters are dealt with outside of court even today?"

"That is correct. But it depends on the merits of the cases concerned."

"That's right. That's right. And isn't it correct that in Mr Ledwidge's case, consideration was given, and serious consideration at that, to having him dealt with administratively?"

"If I remember correctly, that was considered at one stage."

"And there was even talk of an admission of guilt fine and him paying his money and it was only at the last minute that the decision was changed?"

"To be honest, one of the senior officers in charge, without consulting with the Chief Immigration Services, who has subsequently been alleged in corruption charges, decided to take that route. But after consulting with the Chief Immigration Services, he was overruled and the decision was taken for the case to go to court."

"But you'd at least concede that in this case, this form or that form of dealing with it was considered?"

"Yes, as I said, by the senior officer who is now being investigated for corruption charges." The cat was out of the bag and he coughed profusely to a stunned court room. When he composed himself, Mr Howse waited and looked at him fiercely and breaking the silence he said loudly, "Who is that person?"

Naidoo couldn't regain his composure and in a confused state he looked at the ground before looking at the magistrate and said, "I am not sure if I am at liberty to mention his name in court."

No words were spoken, just a reluctant nod from the bench and Naidoo blurted out his name. "Menthe, Terence Menthe." It was as we had suspected, the collaborator of Habib Khan and the mole the Mansoors wanted to expose who nearly jeopardised their corrupt plans.

EIGHTEEN

Descent into 'Guilty plea' by Persuasion

In the midst of unknown fear and frightening death threats to me and members of my family from men whose constant companions were AK47 Kalashnikov assault rifles was terrifying beyond words. The sinister comings and goings of scrupulous corrupt officials and guards who conspired with the perpetrators was unbelievable and beyond imagination.

The scurrilous flea-ridden sponge mattresses used for sleeping and rat-infested cells occupied by deranged individuals with an amalgamation of crimes lived side by side with innocent and petty criminals in a cesspit of inhuman degradation. The fearful imagination of spending two or three years in this colony of a forgotten hellhole, not knowing whether or not I would survive, with constant death threats was outside of my remit. It was upon advice and that of my own counsel that pressurised me into pleading guilty in order to be set free and leave it all behind. My advocate in his wisdom was acutely aware of the dangers lurking within a very corrupt judicial system and tried his best to present a case in the hope that the magistrate might deliver justice.

Following Naidoo's curt admission relating to Terence Menthe, Advocate Jimmy Howse addressed the Court in mitigation. "Your Worship, of course a balanced sentence consists of consideration of the personal circumstances of the accused, weighed against the crime or crimes convicted, and also taking into account the interests of the community. Let's deal with the man before you. He is a 51-year-old first offender. He is a person of some significant standing. The only cogent evidence before you is that he led a crime-free life up to this case. I have handed up the certificates of character from the Irish police and, Your Worship, I submit that those speak very loudly of Mr Ledwidge's past conduct. The fact that a person has reached the age of 51 with a clean record clearly indicates that he is not the sort of person with a propensity to commit crime. It also indicates that his prospects of reforming and completely rehabilitating himself, as a result of this dreadful experience and this case itself, are excellent. In other words, what Your Worship can say with confidence in this matter is that Mr Ledwidge has clearly learned his lesson from what has occurred in this matter. He will no longer be a burden on this country or its people, if a non-custodial sentence is imposed, because he will quite simply be deported back to Ireland where he will remain and it appears that he will have great difficulty returning here again, if ever. Notwithstanding that he has family here, Your Worship, I would ask you to take into account as, in itself, a punishment for Mr Ledwidge in the future because Your Worship has heard that he has a sister here who resides here permanently and obviously he is going to be precluded from visiting his sister in the future.

"In addition to that, Your Worship heard the other day the testimony of Dr Kanjee, which I can submit can be taken into account on sentence here, of the very traumatic effect that detention had.

"Your Worship deals extensively with cases involving dishonesty. Matters involving corruption, fraud, etcetera. We know this case does not fall into that category of offences where a first offender needs to go to jail. Equally, Your Worship, we've established that the other charge and that is the contravention of the immigration laws, is one, which on its own feet does not justify imprisonment for a first offender. I am therefore contending that the crimes themselves are not such as would call for a term of imprisonment and are such where a commensurate fine would be more than adequate punishment as being fitting in all the circumstances.

"Your Worship, when one punishes an offender, one also punishes him for his actual wrongdoings. It emerges from the plea that the accused before you, Your Worship, was not the initiator of any of the misdeeds in this case. I think it is very important that we establish why this crime was committed. The accused wanted to purchase a property and to use that property to run a business in South Africa. He has made no bones about the fact that he wanted to take up permanent residency here and to actually contribute to the economy of the country. We know also that the accused brought in a substantial sum of money for that purpose.

"It is very clear before Your Worship why it was necessary to hasten the application for temporary and, permanent residence. The letters that are exhibited before the Court indicate that the property in question was not available in the medium to long term, but only available for purchase in the very short term. There is the letter from Patricia Lerm, Your Worship, which indicates quite clearly that time was of the essence. If we read that together with the testimony of Chief Inspector Naidoo, we then know why this route was chosen by the person Habib Khan, as opposed to the legal route. Quite simply, because to have taken the legal route would have been approximately a year, which would have been very difficult for the accused to get going with any business dealing, or the purchase of any property and really would have frustrated much of his ends.

"But, Your Worship, even more important than that, is the accused gave mandates to Habib Khan to do things lawfully in order to gain him permission to stay in this country. The accused did not mandate Habib Khan to act unlawfully. It was only at an advanced stage of the process of getting the accused his documents that he realised that fraud had been employed. Your Worship well knows that it is very difficult at that stage for someone to be bold enough to stand up and say, 'Well, I am not going to be part of that.' Certainly he should have, Your Worship. But this is where I am going to ask the Court to look at the element of temptation. We know, like in shoplifting cases for example, and I know this is not perhaps the best comparison, our highest courts have often said that the punishments are severely mitigated because of the extreme temptation. You have goods displayed there basically for the taking and people are tempted to take them. Here the person, Habib Khan, had already set this process in motion. He presented the accused with these documents already prepared and it was in those circumstances where the accused acquiesced to it. So, Your Worship, I am going to ask that the Court consider the degree of temptation involved to be such that it makes the accused's conduct understandable, never justifiable, but understandable. It is also important that once the accused decided to acquiesce, it again wasn't he who personally went and made the misrepresentations. These were all done again by agents and the accused is not the person who actually went up and told the lie. He is not the person who went up and bribed the official. So, Your Worship, those are all very important factors.

"Another important factor in my submission mitigating the sentence is that we can surely accept that if the accused had made his application properly, it would have been accepted. In other words, the accused would certainly have been regarded as a fit and proper person to become a temporary resident of this country. Indeed, Your Worship, I submit on everything that is before you. The indications are strong that the accused would have been welcomed with open arms.

"When imposing punishment, it is always important, Your Worship, to try to put a finger on the mischief that is to be avoided in cases of this sort, is clearly to keep undesirables out of the country and those who are going to basically exploit our country and prejudice within the country. This case is unique that the accused does not fall at all into that category of persons. He instead falls into the category of persons who contribute to the socio-economic development of the country. He is therefore, not one of those persons that, in the evidence of Chief Inspector Naidoo, can be described as the problem that the authorities are trying to solve. Your Worship, that is very important because I suspect that when the prosecutor stands up, she is going to try to appeal to the Court that there is a problem that this country has and is going to try to ask the Court to use the accused as an example to attempt to solve the problem that the country has.

"Now, Your Worship, exemplary sentences we know, by their very nature, are unfair. There is a host of decisions in this regard. Basically, to use an accused as an example is to impose upon him a sentence that is greater than his just deserts and to employ that sentence as a means to deter others from doing similar things. The unfairness would be exacerbated in a case where an accused is used to deter others from doing something that the accused himself hasn't done, or to deter a category of persons into which the accused himself does not fall.

"I am going to ask the Court earnestly not to use the accused as an example. This is not an appropriate case in which to do it. That there is an aggravating or potentially aggravating circumstance, I am going to acknowledge, and that is in the form of Mrs Muniaama Moodley. Having said that, I would ask that the Court carefully assess the extent of aggravation. What happened is that a marriage certificate was fraudulently created or forged, which indicated that the accused was married to Muniaama Moodley. It was put in the accused's documents and put on the official records of the country. It was not included, however, in Muniaama Moodley's documents.

"The legal position is that Muniaama Moodley was never married to the accused and nothing will change that. Therefore, Your Worship, when we look at the implications, we must be very careful and we must accept that Muniaama Moodley could never have been bound by the implications of marriage. In other words, if someone had tried to sue her, she would have an absolute and complete immediate defence, because the marriage was void *ab inito* and accordingly, all of the *sequelae* or consequences of that marriage are not binding on Muniaama Moodley. She was unaware of it, Your Worship, and only became aware of it when the immigration officials knocked on her door. I was very careful in cross-examination to establish from Muniaama Moodley what the actual harm is that she perceived herself to have suffered, and all that she's really been able to say is that she was shocked when she was told of the fact. No, Your Worship, I can read between the lines and I can see what's happened in this case. The State has clearly informed Muniaama Moodley that it's a terrible thing that's happened and she must come to court and she must testify. And, Your Worship, I think that's largely the reason why we saw her demeanour that she displayed in the witness stand this morning.

"I am going to go so far as to suggest that the prosecution or the State, let's put it this way, the State are largely to blame for the position in which Mrs Moodley finds herself. It would have been the duty of those investigators who knocked on her door, if they had done their jobs properly, to have comforted her immediately and to have said to her, 'Mrs Moodley, whether the records say it or not, you are not married to this man. There are no consequences that will flow from this, except that you can carry on with your life and the records will be corrected to reflect the true position.' Your Worship, that this was not done was, in my submission, to elevate the trauma and her concern about this matter and I am going to suggest that she was unfairly employed in *aggravation* of sentence against the accused.

"The demands of the community are very important in a case of this sort. I am going to submit that no member of the community would ever request or require that the accused be jailed. No member of a right thinking community would want this man to go to jail. Even Muniaama Moodley, Your Worship, under oath said that she forgives the accused and now there is the element of forgiveness from the prosecution's witness in aggravation. Even if… if she is prepared to grant such forgiveness, why not the rest of society? I am, therefore, contesting that a sentence of imprisonment is totally out of proportion to the crimes.

"We are basically talking about a temporary residence permit and the marriage certificate. Mr Ledwidge was dispossessed of nearly one million rands [£100,000], by the Mansoors, which is now part of a civil action.

"In closing, I would ask the Court not to be tempted to incarcerate the accused any further by reason of these so-called investigations, which are ongoing. I can tell Your Worship that this issue received close scrutiny by your brother in K Court. In K Court, the Court was persuaded that there is insufficient evidence with which to charge the accused for those offences. The prosecution have had the better part of three weeks in order to investigate those charges and have not come up with anything. We know very well that if there is insufficient evidence to charge a man, then there is really nothing. It would, I submit, be unfair to incarcerate the accused for that reason in order that the prosecution can further their investigations.

"Your Worship, those are my submissions."

The scheming magistrate appeared as though she had been caught in a tangled web, not knowing how to escape.

"Thank you," she replied as she called the prosecutor to address the Court.

"Your Worship, it is clear that the contraventions of the Aliens Control Act has been met in the past with suspended sentences or fines, thereby the enabling the immigration officers to actually deport the accused and not incur any further expenses to keep them in South African jails. However, the evidence of Mr Naidoo has to be taken into account with regard to the deterrent effect that these sentences have in the past imposed for contraventions of the Aliens Control Act and what effect it has had on the country as a whole.

"Your Worship, the effect is that the contraventions have increased and basically the number of aliens coming into the country has become epidemic of sorts. The Court also heard Mr Naidoo's evidence that the problem with aliens is also their involvement in further crimes. Now in this case, the illegal alien before the Court is one such person.

"Now if one looks at the evidence of corruption, Your Worship, it is indeed a very serious offence and I see that my learned friend has not even touched on the seriousness of corruption. This is actually involving the corruption of a Home Affairs official. The Court has just to pick up a newspaper to see the prevalence of corruption within the Department of Home Affairs. In fact, the witness, Mr Naidoo, testified that there has been an arrest with regard to an official just yesterday. It is clear that corruption has become a sort of epidemic within the Department of Home Affairs and the fact is the corruption charges on its own, without fraud, and the contravention of the Aliens Control Act, demands a custodial sentence.

"Now, if one looks at the history of the accused as presented by the defence, it seems that he appears to be somewhat of an eminent character in Ireland and has been active in South Africa as well with regard to Human Rights and gay issues.

"Your Worship, one then begs the question as to why he did not apply for this legally and why he decided to conform to Habib's fraudulent activities of obtaining this marriage certificate in the manner that he did. Now a person of his standing would have no problem acquiring citizenship in this country and permanent residence. When one looks at the offence he is being tried for, he says Khan did everything. The State accepts that. In fact, the State has evidence that there were other people involved in this whole thing and then that leads to the question of a syndicate operating within Home Affairs to ensure that persons like the accused actually gain entry into this country and remain here illegally.

"Your Worship, with regard to the type of offence that has been committed, it is indeed serious and it is prevalent. One has only to look at the evidence of Mr Naidoo just to realise that there are hundreds of cases being investigated, that there are special units that had to be created to deal with the influx of aliens into the country and to deal with their deportation. Then one has to look carefully at his evidence that the person who decided this matter will be dealt with administratively was one Terence Menthe, the very official that has been named as the person who received the bribe. The question of whether that decision to deal with the accused administratively was a valid one. As soon as the State was aware of Mr Menthe's involvement, he was removed off the case and, in fact, Mr Naidoo was asked to oversee this immediately and ensure that Mr Menthe has no further dealings with this case and that he was to be arrested following allegations in this case.

"The question of a proper sentence and the evidence of Mrs Muniaama Moodley and the fact that she was brought to court was to show the Court actually how she was affected by this and the fact that she was shocked, suffered illness as a result of this and had to visit a doctor twice in three weeks to deal with her illness. Your Worship could see that she is clearly a woman who believes in her religion and practises her religion as a devout Tamil person. She goes to the temple. She explained to the Court that a widow does not replace the thali and dot with regard to the religious custom that she follows. And the fact that she is married to a foreign national has become a source of embarrassment to her and her four daughters. And, in fact, she indicated to the Court that she was traumatised by this entire incident.

"Your Worship, it does not become the duty of the immigration officers to actually comfort her, because when they approached her, they did not know that she did not know anything. The question is, it was only at that stage when she denied knowledge of this. She could very well have been one of those South African women that actually assisted the accused in staying in the country. It was only later found out that she knew nothing about this. So, she would have been approached as a suspect and that in itself is traumatising.

"And clearly, Your Worship, this case has indicated to the Court that it is clearly a problem with regards to aliens coming into this country and actually seeking the use of officials, as well as South African citizens, to perpetuate their crimes and their fraudulent activity.

"With regard the accused going back to Ireland begs the question as to why he wants to be deported so quickly without recovering his money from the Mansoors, whom it is alleged defrauded him. The question of the investigation of fraud, the State can and will go ahead with the investigation of fraud and this Court will not be able to sentence the accused and ensure that this investigation is complete and the State will not even ask the Court to do that, because the investigations can continue while the accused is in Ireland.

"The question of an appropriate sentence here, Your Worship, the question of a fine, the State submits, is totally inappropriate. And, therefore, the State will submit that the only suitable sentence here in this case is one of direct imprisonment. Thank you, Your Worship."

The question of "further investigations" relating to fraud, that I was a member of an illegal organisation or part of a syndicate was a fabrication of the truth and absurd. It was preposterous to suggest that I would align myself in such criminal activity as I would have been clueless as to its operations and what purpose would it have served? Similarly, it was well known in Ireland that I was gay and I was gaining prominence in South Africa, where it would have been unintelligent to engage in a bogus marriage scam. They were ruthless in their efforts to prevent me suing them for the monies they had literally stolen from me through their fraudulent means.

Their main aim was to prevent me from issuing civil proceedings or exposing their alleged association with Buthelezi, Minister of Home Affairs, Jackie Selebe, Chief of Police and Penuell Maduna, Minister for Justice and Constitutional Development and their associates. It is ironic not coincidental, that Terence Menthe was arrested, whilst the 'Mansoors' were never apprehended and to this day the authorities in South Africa have refused to touch them.

The magistrate referred the matter to the following Monday for sentencing but in the meantime Mr Howse addressed the Court in closing.

"Your Worship, as far as the corruption charges are concerned, my learned friend's made much of imprisonment being the only appropriate sentence for corruption. Obviously and, firstly each case is judged on its merits and secondly, when dealing with corruption, one always has the corruptor and the corruptee. I cannot think of a case where the corruptor, in other words that's the person who pays the bribe, has been sent to imprisonment, apart from one or two cases involving excessively large amounts of money. I cannot certainly think of any case involving approximately 11,000 rands, [£1,100], where the corruptor did the corruption through the medium of another, where it would ever be said that imprisonment is the proper option for a 51-year-old first offender. So, Your Worship, I feel the prosecution has really blown the whole corruption issue out of all proportion and that society would certainly not demand a prison sentence for that level of corruption by a corruptor.

"And, Your Worship, the Tamil issue. I don't want to belittle any religion or to make any adverse comment there, but unless I misunderstood things, all that the complainant, Mrs Moodley, said is that she suffered some embarrassment because of that. If we look at this very carefully, what does she have to be embarrassed about? Somebody took advantage of her and she really is the innocent victim of circumstance. Her religion, Your Worship, would never hold anything of that sort against her. Indeed, I submit, every religion, including the Tamil religion, would be sympathetic of a victim like Mrs Moodley and would not have any reason to condemn her, or to prejudice her in any way in her religion. So, much of that, Your Worship.

"And then my learned friend made the point, which might be an aggravating circumstance, that when the officials approached Mrs Moodley, she was regarded as a suspect. Your Worship, if that was the case, then of course it would be prejudicial to a person. It is ridiculous for the following reason. When Mrs Moodley was involved in a marriage of convenience by consent and could be regarded as a suspect, it would have been found out within the first couple of seconds. I am telling you now what would have happened here is that the immigration officials would have asked her for her ID book and in that ID book would have been a marriage certificate and there would have been a properly registered marriage. She probably would have taken the surname Ledwidge on and it would have been an entirely different situation. So, Your Worship, that argument does not even begin to lend itself to our facts and I submit that the moment the immigration officers interviewed her and asked her for her ID, it would have been immediately apparent to them that there was no marriage of convenience by consent. I think that really underscores my argument.

"This is not the case in which to impose direct imprisonment. As the prosecutor pointed out, the only ground to do it is on grounds of deterrence and she mentioned that fraud was rife and corruption is rife. But, Your Worship, other forms of fraud and corruption are also rife. There are dozens of fraud cases before the courts every day and the norm in sentencing is that when it's fraud involving a first offender and it's not involving a massive amount of money, that offender gets the benefit of a non-custodial sentence. This case is no different from those and I'd ask Your Worship to apply those principles. Thank you."

The magistrate looked at me for the first time with a gentle smile and said, "The Court is adjourned until Monday 13 May 2002 and the detention of the accused is the same; Chatsmed Gardens Hospital."

I sensed that the magistrate was being kind to me as if to say, "Everything will be alright."

Me in South Africa in the late 1980s.

Me & Tony – South Africa, 1987

Outside frontage of The Horse & Carriage

**Danny La Rue and me at the opening of The Horse & Carriage.
23 September 1993**

Another moment on opening night with the press.

The Horse & Carriage brochure.

DUBLIN
CHAMBER
of Commerce

THE
BUSINESS FACE
OF DUBLIN

AWARDS
1993

HIGHLY COMMENDED

THE HORSE AND CARRIAGE
Aungier Street

The simple facade of the Horse and Carriage in Aungier Street is an example of what can be achieved with a little sensitivity to the environment. It lifts the overall appearance of the street with careful and colourful maintenance and design

Sponsored by

Award Winning

**Dublin Chamber of Commerce Award
1993**

**The Horse & Carriage ready for the St Patrick's Day parade
17 March 1993**

**Danny and me making history
as the only two gay men in the St. Patrick's Day Parade
representing The Horse & Carriage.**

Former British footballer/Irish soccer manager Jack Charlton,
Me, Danny and Tony

The truth is out – poster of my book.

OUT OF AFRICA

Having been imprisoned in a disease-riddled, overcrowded prison, the victim of violence, threats, intimidation and an allegedly corrupt South African legal system, Liam Ledwidge is a man with a shocking story to tell, as **Ciara McGrattan** finds out.

You may not have heard of him but in the '90s Liam Ledwidge was the co-owner of Ireland's first gay hotel, The Horse and Carriage on Dublin's Aungier Street. With its basement sauna, the H&C hit the tabloid headlines in 1994 when it burned down and a priest was evacuated wearing just a towel.

After those events Ledwidge moved to post-apartheid South Africa, where, with the help of a reputable foreign investments company he found a suitable location for a new business venture and began the process of legally obtaining a visa. Unfortunately, not everyone involved in the transaction was to be trusted and Ledwidge believes he fell victim to the machinations of an unscrupulous quadriplegic con man, one of the powerful Mansoor family who had been long-standing friends of the South African branch of Ledwidge's family. According to Ledwidge, the Mansoors extorted hundreds of thousands of pounds from him and led to his eventual imprisonment at Westville, one of the most notoriously dangerous and overcrowded prisons on the planet. To ensure he wouldn't start civil proceedings against them in order to recoup his money, Ledwidge believes Mansoor family needed leverage and so turbwknownt to

him involved him in a false marriage to a South African woman. Several officials involved in the case have since been sacked - most notably Police Chief and Head of Interpol Jackie Selebi, who was arrested on suspicion of links to organised crime.

On advisement, under assurances that a guilty plea would mean a swift deportation for him, and at gunpoint, Ledwidge plead guilty to faking a marriage certificate. "We were told that if we hadn't plead guilty we could've been waiting ten years for the case to be heard," he says, now in the comfort of a Dublin city centre café.

By the time he pleaded guilty, he had already been imprisoned at Westville for several weeks by delay tactics. Sexually assaulted, starved, beaten up and packed in cells with up to 200 men, many of whom were on their last legs, dying of Aids, he knew what endless incarceration while waiting for trial would mean. However, his guilty plea backfired and

GCN – Review of my book
Dangerous People Dancing Incognito.
2008

How I brought down South Africa's most corrupt police chief

Corkman vows to continue his fight to expose crime in the country's force

Cormac McQuinn

THE IRISHMAN who exposed South Africa's corrupt former police chief Jackie Selebi vowed last night to continue his fight against graft in the country's police force, saying: 'It's no good just taking him out. You've got to remove all the cancer.'

The news that South Africa's top policeman has been convicted for consorting with powerful gangsters and that he took bribes from criminals was reported around the world, but few have told the story of the central role played by Paul O'Sullivan.

In November, the Irish Mail on Sunday revealed Mr O'Sullivan's most decade-long battle to expose the crimes of South Africa's top policeman and the shocking attempts by gunmen to silence him.

You've got to remove all the cancer'

On Friday, he attended the final hearing in a Johannesburg court where his nemesis was convicted of corruption. An emotional Mr O'Sullivan, cried out: 'Shame on you, Selebi! Shame on you!' at the end of the nine-month trial investigating the police chief's corrupt relationship with South African gangster Glenn Agliotti.

Yesterday, after a night 'partying' with the prosecution team, Mr O'Sullivan told the MoS his battle would continue as it's still not safe for his wife and six children to return to South Africa.

'They're still in hiding,' he said. 'I say it'll be another year or two before they can come back.'

He explained: 'Unfortunately this man [Selebi] was in office for eight years so what I now have to

SNARED: Former police chief Jackie Selebi leaves court

DOGGED: Paul O'Sullivan spent years on the case

do is take out all the people he appointed. It's no good just taking him out. You've got to remove all the cancer.'

The trial came about after Mr O'Sullivan, a former MI6 spy and later head of security for South Africa's airports, compiled a 140-page dossier on Selebi's extensive corruption that included receiving €110,000 and numerous gifts from shady underworld figures in return for preferential treatment by the police.

Mr O'Sullivan was prompted to launch a personal investigation against Mr Selebi after the former police chief had him sacked from his job as group executive for aviation security for Airports Company of South Africa (ACSA).

'Fire in his belly kept him going'

Born in Tipperary, Mr O'Sullivan was reared in poverty in rural Cork and was, as he tells it, toughened up by a harsh father and casual cruelty in the local CBS.

He ran away at the age of 14 and eventually wound up in London, where he joined the British Army and later MI6.

He moved to South Africa over a decade ago and took the job as airport security chief in 2001 before being sacked at Selebi's behest in 2003, just after the ACSA had paid him a good performance bonus.

The Irishman, who in the course of his investigation survived three attempts on his life, had been trying to clean up South Africa's airports, trying to end rampant drug and people smuggling as well as disciplining widespread corruption within the airports' security guards.

After Selebi's conviction for corruption, Mr O'Sullivan said: 'The final score is South Africa 1, Selebi 0. Our country wins, Selebi loses.'

He credited his considerable stamina in pursuing the long investigation down to his being Irish and the 'fire in his belly'.

The film rights to his story have been sold to an independent Hollywood producer with Mr O'Sullivan envisioning Liam Neeson or Tommy Lee Jones playing him.

cormac.mcquinn@mailonsunday.ie

JuLY 4th 2010 - MAiL oN SuNDAY

**Jackie Selbi, Chief of Police, South Africa
Convicted of corruption.**

**My dear friend Ann, and me.
On our way to the Aran islands June 2018**

My dear friend celebrity priest Joe McDonald.

NINETEEN

Shattering Sentencing

Following the magistrate's ruling that sentence would be passed on Monday, I was allowed to stroll through the court house and out onto the street with Colin Bigela accompanying me at every step with his hand on his gun at all times. A student shouted, "It's a charade, man! It's all a charade."

We were waiting at the side of the van on the main street awaiting Alpheus Sibila when Bigela made the snide comment, "You're a fine target for a hitman," and for once I agreed with him as I looked around at the sprawling glass buildings and wondered if that was the idea. If it was, there was nothing I could do about it.

I once again climbed into the wagon alone as Sibila and Bigela sat in the front, with two extra cars following behind until they eventually pulled into the parking space in front of the Department of Home Affairs on Umgeni Road. I was then left in the back of the wagon for the best part of an hour.

Then they came out laughing and joking and staring contemptuously through the window at me, as though I were an animal in a cage. We eventually left for Chatsworth Police Station with another unidentified official travelling with us, as I was being transferred to my police guard who would accompany me back to the hospital.

My family and friends comforted me for the weekend and I was confident that I would be back in Ireland within a few days. On Monday 13 May 2002, I awoke at 5am and left for the court at 10am as we had received notice that a verdict would be given earlier than expected. We arrived into the large court complex where the public were already gathering. I noticed the State Prosecutor deep in conversation with reporters who had not been in the court on the Friday. When the Court assembled, she stood, sporting her usual smirk and made sure that we all heard her as she bellowed like a ringmaster at a circus, "The matter is for sentence, Your Worship."

The magistrate, dressed in pink with matching lipstick opened by saying, "Mr Ledwidge, in coming to an appropriate sentence, the court normally takes into consideration the relevant factors of your personal circumstances, the seriousness of the offence, as well as the interests of society. All these are then weighed up and a suitable sentence arrived at. Now, with regard to your personal circumstances, the court accepts what the accused has said in mitigation of sentence that he has a blemish free record in Ireland, being 51-years-old, single and a champion of gay rights, both in Ireland and South Africa. The court also accepts that he has brought considerable amounts of money and friends into South Africa.

"On the other hand, however, Exhibits H is an interdict that Mr Mansoor specifically obtained citing the accused, as the first respondent, 'be restrained from directly or indirectly assaulting, verbally abusing or threatening, intimidating or harassing or interfering with the complainant, Mr Mansoor.'

"The court also has no cogent reason for why the accused did not make proper application through the correct channels for his residence permit. With regard to the seriousness of the offence, all three offences are regarded in a very serious light by this court. With regard to count one, the Aliens Control Act specifically makes provision for stiff sentences for persons found in the Republic after the expiry of their permit. This is in order to stem the flow and control the number of illegal aliens entering the country, who in turn create various socio-economic problems. The interests of society must also be considered and the South African community has come to view these foreigners in a hostile light, as they usurp employment in basic communities. Furthermore, they have been involved in criminal activities on behalf of international cartels or syndicates.

"The fraud perpetrated by the accused in count two has serious repercussions for Mrs Moodley, although the defence has argued that this is not so. The Court is aware that a person of strong religious faith, such as Mrs Moodley, will feel immense embarrassment and humiliation if her close community discovers that she is married, especially to a white foreigner. Furthermore if she loses her identity document and requests a new one, or should she apply for a passport and visa, she will be reflected as a married person, a fact that cannot be explained away. Such victim of circumstance is now saddled with consequences beyond her control and which she must now undo. The fact that she forgave the accused was an act done after repeated questioning by the defence and her trauma was evident to the Court.

"In spite of knowing the requirements of how to go about applying for residency, he hands to Khan 47,000 rands [£4,700 in those days]. Although the accused found out about Khan's underhand methods, he nevertheless kept silent and hands over 11,500 rands [£1,150 in those days] in order to bribe an official at the Department of Home Affairs. This corruption perpetrated by the accused is, in the court's view, the most heinous of all three offences. The officials of a government department are expected to be above approach. However, the media recently has been indulged with reports of corrupt officials who, in exchange for money, issue falsified certificates. Society's reprehensible attitude at those that perpetrate these offences must be reflected in the sentences that the courts impose. The public has a vital interest in the honesty and integrity of the officials of any branch of the public service. No departure from the strictest standards of honesty and integrity can be tolerated.

"When the Court balances all the relevant factors in this case, it concludes that the offences are so serious, and in respect of the imposition of sentence for which society has a substantial interest, that the personal circumstances of the accused, although they cannot be ignored, recede somewhat in importance. The Court is of the view, therefore, that the deterrent aspect of sentence must come to the fore and an element of example must feature in his sentence. You are therefore sentenced as follows: in respect of count one, the accused is sentenced to 5000 rands [£500], or twelve months' imprisonment. Counts two and three are taken together for the purpose of sentence and the accused is sentenced to three years' imprisonment."

In a stunned and silent courtroom, a litany of illegal irregularities had occurred where the magistrate had chosen to ignore the wisdom of Advocate Howes and allowed senselessness to override sensibility. Every word she spoke reminded me of the Mansoors and when she uttered extractions from the interdict, we knew then that the eagle had landed and was being well fed. The interdict was grossly full of untruths and lies as these incidents never took place and the document wasn't worth the paper it was written on. It was shambolic injustice from a corrupt court who preferred the testimony of a thief, a fraudster and a conman. He conspired with others and the magistrate was acutely aware of that and I wouldn't be surprised if they had written her delivery speech.

It was a grave miscarriage of justice against creed, colour, gender and sexual orientation. It had the classical hallmarks of a prejudicial, biased, corrupt and non-compromising judicial system.

As the eyes of the court room stared at the magistrate and the State Prosecutor who smiled when the verdict was given, Advocate Howse said, "I would request, Your Worship, that the accused be detained here as we are most definitely noting an appeal against the sentence. Your Worship, I will be bringing an application for bail pending an appeal. May the accused be retained in court; we will just be a few minutes?"

"Yes, certainly," she murmured reluctantly.

Advocate Howse stood and addressed the Court, "Your Worship, I have prepared a notice of Appeal and there is also an accompanying Power of Attorney from the accused. The accused is going to be noting an appeal against all the sentences, but obviously in particular the term of imprisonment. If I may hand up the notice of appeal and the accompanying Power of Attorney?"

"Yes, certainly."

I was called into the witness box and was asked for my full name and I confirmed that I was appealing against the sentences imposed. I also agreed that upon advice I was seeking bail pending the outcome of the appeal. However, I knew that this would not be granted. It was my duty to inform them as to where I would be staying and once again verify that the people with whom I would be staying were my sister and brother-in-law.

They argued about the issue of the Irish Embassy willing to assist in giving me an emergency passport so that I could carry ID. The prosecution objected, saying that I would be a flight risk and had the ridiculous notion that we could call upon Habib Khan for assistance. This was a man who owed me 47,000 rands (£4700 in those days), whilst the police were allegedly in search of him and she suggested that we would contact him. To our knowledge, he had either fled, or the Mansoors were hiding him.

The legal shambles had to be seen to be believed, as a highly questionable State Magistrate and an inexperienced State Prosecutor succumbed to their own egotistical desires for power, money and social elevation. It was a thundering disgrace to the cloth of the legal profession.

The State Prosecutor went on to promulgate the syndicate of cartels, which they alleged I was part and parcel of. I was sick to my stomach and completely shattered and dumbfounded as one wretched lie after the other was told. I began to question my own being and existence. The revolting untruths caused me a lot of pain. She made me feel like an outcast, a leper in society, the scum of the earth. She reminded her friend, the magistrate, that I was a *persona non grata* and that I had no standing in the courts.

She went on, "Your Worship, with regards to appeals, it is clear that the High Courts will only interfere with a sentence when there has been a misdirection by the Court. The High Courts have held that the sentencing of an accused is actually primarily within the discretion of the Trial Court and the State submits that, in this instance, there has been no misdirection by the Court and, therefore the prospects of success on appeal, the State submits are not very good."

She was stating by her own conviction that the Appeal Court would not be favourable to my plea and how wrong and embarrassed she would find herself months later when the magistrate and the State Prosecutor were both castigated by the Court of Appeal.

The Mansoors had achieved what they set out to do and their wishes were granted by a Court of amicable agreement. The magistrate in her final delivery, shouted so that she could be heard in the bleak courtroom, "Mr Ledwidge, the Court has heard what you have had to say with regard to the application for bail pending appeal and also what the prosecutor and Mr Howes have had to say. The Court is of the opinion that any other court would not give you a non-custodial sentence. In the circumstances, bail pending appeal is refused."

I was eventually escorted by the guards to a lift to descend to the waiting cells beneath the courts for transportation to the disreputable Westville Prison. One of the lifts was broken, forcing us to take another one on a main floor and as we entered, there standing in front of me was the blushing magistrate. As the door opened on the next floor, the burly prosecutor entered, greeting the magistrate. Not realising that I was present, she turned to the magistrate and said, "We should have invited overseas' press," at which point the magistrate coughed and blushed with embarrassment and said she needed to get out on the next floor. It was the last time I ever saw them both and I calmly thought of their shameful and underhanded conduct.

I was taken into 'the cage' where multiple amounts of black and Indian prisoners were awaiting transportation back to prison. Apart from myself there was only one other young white lad there. They looked forlorn and rejected, but I had to realise that most of them were ruthless dangerous men and could not be trusted.

It was like a flash of lightning when the young white male was quickly ushered into an unlocked antechamber, where he was gagged and stripped below the waist, before three of them raped him. It was yet again another rape I was to witness over the coming months. They used no condoms and when they were finished, the last thing the victim would do was complain. He merely sobbed a little as he pulled his trousers up around his waist.

These young reprehensible men of violence and sexual perversion knew no better and their sexual urges were not borne of homosexuality, but rather basic animalistic thuggery. They procured rape not only as a favourite pastime, but they saw it as a virile exercise in proving a 'macho' image amongst the thugs who were their fellow inmates and members of the notorious gangs. Because there were no females about, the more vulnerable the victim, the higher chance he had of being raped. The authorities were acutely aware of what was going on, but if it kept the inmates quiet, as with smoking dagga, then it made life easier for them.

They were taken out in groups and as the day rolled on, I was still waiting. I soon realised that I was alone in the large cell, with no fellow inmates or guards. My lawyer Pregasen Marimuthu was later to write, "Our client was not transferred to Westville prison on the 13 May 2002, as stipulated on his detention warrant, but he was held overnight in the Durban Court holding cells without food, water or supervision." We can speculate all day and night as to why this happened but to this day no one knows why.

I had taken my jacket off and I tried sleeping on a bench within the large cell, but found it difficult. It was freezing cold and I was extremely thirsty, but I had become used to the denial of water from the South African authorities. I could tell the time from a clock in the distance and I could hear the drone of traffic outside of the building.

As night approached, the silence that befell the place was comforting as I tried to rest for the night without success. I fell asleep at one point but awoke suddenly, startled by cold hands touching my body and jumped to my feet. Two black men, whom I later discovered were prisoners, were taken there to clean the cells. I walked into the light of the main cell, where an astounded officer was baffled as to why I had not been taken to Westville prison the previous day. He kindly gave me a welcome cup of coffee and was extremely friendly towards me. It was 5.45am as the two prisoners, with brushes in hand, beckoned for me to give them a cigarette. I lit a cigarette as they grabbed it from my hand and gazed aimlessly, not knowing what fate lay ahead.

TWENTY

Utter Bowels of Hell-Rape-Disease-Bloodshed and Suicide.

The large prison van capable of carrying twenty prisoners or more, was parked in the underground roadway of the court's prison enclosure. A sea of nearly two hundred black faces highlighted by their white teeth, stared curiously at this white man being led into the prison wagon. A well-dressed foreigner looking like a symbol of authority and being led away as a common criminal was beyond their comprehension. The white man, no matter what their inner fears or hatred of him, was seen as power, even in this predominantly black-governed country.

It was the psychological effect of years of oppression and apartheid that had some conditioned in this way. The Dutch, British and Germans along with many other European states had conquered and raped this land centuries ago. With the gold and diamond reserves, they had built an empire of wealth and subdued its people through segregation. The black man was always the underdog in his own country and with only eight years of power behind him, found it difficult to comprehend. They craved the status and education of the white man, but in their young hearts they knew it was never in the offing. The haggard faces and poorly-clad bodies shielded by the cell bars were indicative of their poverty, which resulted with incarceration for their crimes. There were young and barefooted prisoners, mere mites of twelve years of age, mixed with toughened hardened teenagers they viewed as icons.

I entered the long gloomy prison van, alone with my thoughts and felt their eyes follow my every move as the door banged behind me. It smelled like an abhorrent drug den, with its panels decorated in graffiti. As the large prison wagon pulled out from its enclosure into the midday sun, I could see the slogans written on the panels: ***"NO PAIN NO GAIN – MOTHER FUCKERS WE ARE WAITING FOR YOU AT WESTVILLE."*** The colloquial scribbles and diagrams of sexual connotations were rife in the filthy wagon. I wondered if Christ was forewarning me, as the teachings of my youth within the Roman Catholic Church were at the forefront of my mind. My faith was spiritual and physical crouch in the midst of so much adversity and surrounded by so much danger. Within the great walls of isolation, the world would vanish and I was about to enter another time zone of unforgettable horror.

We arrived within the prison grounds as shackled prisoners were being taken to court, their bandaged wounds and scarred faces a frightening sight as armed prison officers stood with ferocious guard dogs and the prisoners eyed me from head to toe. I was never handcuffed or shackled, which remains a mystery to me today, but my spirit was thwarted in a desperate situation of isolation and fear. The Home Affairs' officials had constantly reminded me of my fate and now the corrupt officers were doing the same, often at the butt of a gun. They frequently reminded me that they would execute their threats without entertaining a thought if I did not cooperate with them, even inside the prison.

The guard was an obnoxious individual who hurried me through the gleaming polished doors and reception area, a façade to impress visitors. Once I was handed over to the prison authorities, I was escorted through various gates, each clanging behind me, which was a grim reminder of where I was. I thought of the Irish writer Brendan Behan and his auld triangle, which went jingle, jangle, except in place of the jingle jangle were the taunting whistles of the inmates.

I arrived into a bleak hallway where a stout Indian man with missing teeth looked at me as if I had two heads. I thought of the things we used to say about people like him back home: 'Toothless and fruitless', except this was no laughing situation.

"Hee, hee, hee what have we got here?" He giggled, as a cute but nervous inmate took my fingerprints. He kept apologising for his mistakes and I later found out that these tasks were given to trusted prisoners, although their application to work was questionable. I waited for my papers to be processed by the giggling Indian and was told by another comical looking guard with prominent teeth to wait in an unsanitary side room, with broken chairs and dirt-encrusted walls. Through barred windows, I could see overgrown minute wasteland covered with debris thrown from the overhead cells. Vacant-faced prisoners in green uniforms wandered around aimlessly, but I guess I looked no better at times. I felt like a zombie, oblivious to what was going on around me and finding it hard to digest the reality of the nightmare. This was like a scene from a movie, but there was no glitz and glamour, just the depressing surroundings of a forbidden prison and the worst was yet to come.

I was issued with a pink prison card and was taken by another two stern-looking guards through more gates and hallways to another section. Here I was stripped of my clothing as they hustled for a suitably-sized green uniform. I stretched into a damp, green tunic, taken from the end of a barrel, which had been a resting bed for cockroaches and was disgustingly filthy and crawling with lice. I was abruptly told to wait until lockup at 2pm.

I walked nervously towards my appointed cell and waited outside in the crowded, caged yard, which housed many other cells. This was my first glance of the murderers, rapists, drug lords and many other criminals who comprised the family of inmates. There was no differentiation or segregation between prisoners at Westville; they all shared the one house, including the dangerous and often melancholy schizophrenics.

The HIV/AIDS' virus was visibly rampant amongst the lost souls of this Southern African institution, as watery eyes, streaming noses and prominent-boned bodies clad in lice-ridden garments walked aimlessly around the prison yard. Paedophiles stared lustfully as they caught sight of young children being ushered to another part of the prison. As they disappeared from sight, their eyes focused on the young men, now my fellow prisoners on the wing. Their eyes were full of lustful tears, bulging with excitement and their mouths were drooling in anticipation of their forbidden company as they watched the young boys.

The toughened blacks were arguing viciously with two softly-spoken Indians over a dagga (cannabis) deal, which was verging on a violent attack, when a tall handsome Indian man intervened. Several words were spoken and an air of calmness prevailed. The gang dispersed and the handsome Indian looked at me as I smoked a cigarette. He eventually strode in my direction with his hand outstretched and said, "Hi, I'm Peter."

We began talking about our respective cases. Peter was a charming man and although younger than I, he had an air of natural fatherly love. He was known as the drug baron of Ladysmith, which is 236 kilometres from Durban. He had been caught with his twin brother Nigel in a multi-billion rands' bust by the Criminal Assets Bureau, which left him bereft of several houses, Mercedes cars, recording studios, farms, jewellery, a helicopter and a luxurious mansion, which included its own golf course. He didn't mind in the least telling me about this and was proud to say that he had featured on the evening television news.

Peter and his brother were sentenced to life imprisonment. Life imprisonment in South Africa means until death do we part. It was a shivering conversation but I wasn't going to voice my disapproval as I needed all the friends I could get.

Peter was a fitness fanatic and had organised his own weights by filling litres of plastic containers with water, four tied on each side of a brush pole, adequate for training. I was to share an overcrowded cell with Peter, his friend Max and 85 other prisoners. The cell was adequate for 25 people. There was no mattress on the floor for me, so Peter obligingly suggested that I share with him. Once again, it was reminiscent of the previous section and we all had to share the one open toilet and hand wash basin situated in full view of everyone. It was indescribable and humiliating. The cockroach infestation swarmed the one antiquated television set.

There were four other Indians amongst the black prisoners in the cell, who kept to themselves and who disliked white people. I was the only white person in the cell and indeed on that entire wing of overcrowded cells. It later transpired that the four Indians had robbed a bank and killed a white man. Their sentence was 85 years. A black 21-year-old was serving a month for stealing a chicken to feed his family! He too was placed amongst the murderers and rapists and barely slept, having been raped on three occasions.

Peter and Max were very friendly towards me and introduced me to a very charismatic guy named Robert. Robert organised a sponge mattress for me to lie on and Peter gave me one of his sheets and a pillow. I felt a little more at ease but never complacent.

The weather had changed drastically as is the norm in Durban and the rain was dancing against the prison cell, with the foul smell of dagga filling the air as dusk fell upon us. As I lay on my pillow, an army of thoughts invaded my mind. I was acutely aware of the massive press coverage my case had generated, with some headlines describing it, "Gay Alien Gets Jail." I wondered how long it would be before it began to filter through to the other prisoners.

Homosexuality was rampant at Westville, but was used by the gangs for means of prostitution rackets and it was here that I was to see the gangs of 26-year-olds and 28-year-olds in the battle of the bodies!

Homosexuality was considered a necessary silent evil to the prisoners as part of human nature, but only privately within the confines of prison. One would not dare refer to them as 'gay' or 'queer' and some prisoners had a vicious streak of homophobic madness about them. The common use of the word 'rape' noticeably referred to the thugs who were members of the prevalent gangs who raped other prisoners.

There was a terrifying bolt of lightning, accompanied by torrential rain, similar to what one would witness in a dramatic horror movie. I was oblivious to a fight at the end of the cell, until a scuffle left me pinned to the floor as two black guys were pushed on top of me in the melee. I managed to struggle free to witness a ferocious fight between four blacks, their dark bloodied bodies barely visible in the dimly lit cell. Their clothing was torn apart and they spoke in tongues of fire in their native Xhosa, which is the spoken word of the Bantu people of the Cape Province. I was terrified. There was no obvious escape, no protection and no alarm bells to ring. Both gates were locked, with no emergency plan to evacuate in the event of fire.

I tried to sleep after the disturbance when Peter jumped to his feet to apprehend a black guy with a sharpened stick prowling alongside me. There was such a commotion that all of the prisoners jumped to their feet in what appeared to be a volatile situation. Peter pinned the black man to the ground, his face embedded into the sharpness of the concrete floor, with blood gushing profusely from his head and down the side of his face.

"What are you up to Kaffer?" he whispered into his ear, as he pulled his head upwards.

There was no reply. Peter waited and eventually slammed the left side of his face aggressively towards the wall, with blood squirting like a thwarted tap, staining the wall and floor. In an immediate burst of energy, Peter lifted him off his feet to another part of the cell, pushing prisoners to one side in the purge, demanding an answer from the black man. His shaking, blood-drenched body was thrown towards the wall of the cell as the rain continued its descent on the outside. The black man messed himself as his head bounced off the wall. Peter finally warned him that if he did not tell him what was going on, he would make him eat every piece of his vile excrement. It was a heart-stopping, sadistic drama.

The attacker, already in a dire state, struggled to speak as the red blood fell into his mouth in stark contrast to his white teeth. He was carted to the front of the cell by the one toilet bowl and wash basin, where I was unable to hear the verbal transactions. At least an hour had passed when Peter returned. "Go to sleep," he said. "We'll talk later."

It became apparent that the Mansoors had kept their promise and their presence was now felt within the walls at Westville. Out of the blue, a prisoner was given a bloody nose and a brawl ensued, with more trouble, more banging, more screaming and more tension as another day began in earnest.

In a deep state of depression, one prisoner named Sham told me, "I would rather be thrown to the crocodiles than serve the remainder of my twelve years. With the sentences handed down and no rehabilitation, the system is wrong. Instead of living with lepers, I would rather hang myself," and sadly he did.

This suicide affected me greatly and I began to question myself as to what I might have been able to do. I became totally introverted and I felt isolated from normal society. I sat in the open yard with my elbow on my knee and my hand to my forehead when suddenly I felt a soft hand on my shoulder. It was a young Zulu inmate and when I looked at him, he had an angelic face and said, "Don't be sad, nothing lasts forever, think of who you are, you are a person like me. I am somebody, you are somebody." I stared at him as he walked away almost into the abyss. He had being delivering oranges which was a monthly treat for inmates. I have no doubt about it, he saved my life and I will be eternally grateful.

At 3am, we were awoken by the sound of shouting. The doors opened, the lights went on and more prisoners were coming into the already overcrowded cell from Pollsmoor Prison en route to another prison. Pollsmoor was the prison near Cape Town where Nelson Mandela spent his remaining years after leaving Robben Island.

I was suffocating and the foul odours in the sweltering heat of the cell gave rise to prisoners vomiting, which added to the stench. I never once saw detergents used at the prison. The floor of the cell was brushed every morning and washed over with water, but this exercise should have been repeated many times during the day. The entire prison needed to be fumigated.

One morning I walked out into the yard with another prisoner named Charlie, who was 22 years old. He was serving twelve months for stealing shoes for his two children. He seemed a reasonably intelligent young man who was touting prisoners for 'wash jobs', which meant he would wash your vest for a cigarette, or any other items for that matter. As we walked in the yard, someone beckoned him and he told me to follow him, which I did to my regret. We entered the last cell on the wing where one prisoner kept guard on the door and six others were inside smoking dagga. Two prisoners immediately arrested Charlie by both of his arms and out from beneath a bunk bed came another handsome Indian, who stared at me and looked at Charlie.

"Where is it, pretty face?" he said to him.

"I haven't got it," he replied.

"The white man, he has it, yes?"

I did not know what was going on and attempted to make my way out when they grabbed hold of me and searched my pockets. When my prison card was the only item they found, he ordered them to strip search me in the most undignified manner. I was trembling with fear. I saw the tears in Charlie's eyes as they held his arms backwards and squeezed his testicles. I was immediately told to put my clothes on as they stripped Charlie naked. The chief interrogator brutally raped him, with one hand around his mouth and the other around his genitals, whilst a sheepish looking black prisoner guarded the entrance to the cell, occasionally glancing in at the brutal rape, which seemed to excite him.

After Charlie's ordeal, we were both released and as we walked back to our cell, I looked at him consumed with pain. With tears in his eyes he told me not to mention it to the other prisoners. It transpired that he owed them money for dagga and he had failed to pay them. He told me that if he didn't pay them within a week, he would not only be raped by the six of them, but he would also receive a severe beating. The only means he had at his disposal to raise cash was to undertake 'wash jobs' or sell a lot more dagga to the over 28s, who had the money from their illegal operations in conjunction with the members of the prison. The stories that I had heard of the place were far worse than I ever had imagined. Charlie vanished overnight and we were never told of his whereabouts.

It was approaching the World Cup in Japan when famous Irish footballer/Manchester United player Roy Keane had the much-publicised row with the then Manager of the Republic of Ireland team, Mick McCarthy. It appeared as though some prisoners were deliberately spoiling for a fight and taunted me over the incident in an attempt to aggravate me, but I attempted to ignore them.

It was 1pm on a Friday when I was told that I was being moved to a different cell on a different wing. I was disappointed as I had become acquainted with Peter and Max and now I had to start all over again. I went with twenty other black prisoners out of the ground floor cells, up the winding caged stairwell and through another set of iron-barred gates to an outer yard, which was caged with steel girders and protective wiring. We were told to sit on our haunches alongside a wall, as members sat leisurely at a wooden desk in the afternoon sunshine. We were carrying lice-inhabited blankets and the stench in the heat was gut-wrenchingly overpowering.

A tall young man in a green overall brushed past the members and began to take all our prison cards for registration to the new wing. I noticed his eyes staring at me and when he took my card he asked, "Irish?" and I nodded.

"Roy Keane, Mick McCarthy. Man, you're going to win."

I was relieved that he saw our boys as heroes and I thanked him for his vote of confidence. He introduced himself as Logan, better known as "Bull". He whistled to one of his fellow inmates whilst taking the crawling mattress and blanket from me and told the inmate to get rid of it, as the accompanying prisoners looked on. Bull had one week left of a ten-year sentence and he was in charge of B401 where I was taken and where I was to remain during my incarceration.

I was introduced to the immediate 'family' namely Ravi, Baboo and Brendan. With Bull being so fascinated with football and well-versed on the Irish squad, I became an instant hit with him. He was in awe of Roy Keane. They noticed that I was in agony with my back pain and so Baboo kindly gave me the bottom bunk bed to lie and sleep. He was a charming guy, who constantly reminded me that he was a 'crook'. He would storm, "Why the hell have those bastards sent you here, those fucking crooks."

Ravi, who was next in line to Bull and who ultimately took over, had originally been sentenced to 95 years' imprisonment for shooting dead three men and dumping their bodies into the Indian Ocean off Durban. On appeal, his sentence was reduced to 30 years. In his heads of argument for the Appeal Court, which he showed me, I saw photographs of all three dead bodies with the open bullet wounds and their grotesque empty eye sockets, which the pathologist suggested had been "plucked and eaten by fish." It seemed that the perpetrators' intention was to allow the bodies to float out to sea, in the hope that they would be devoured by sharks. It was horrifying and difficult to comprehend that such a seemingly sane and kind man could be such a brutal murderer.

Once again the stench and free flow of smoke from dagga was severely irritating, especially to my eyes, but as there was nothing I could do about it, I simply had to live with it. I had tried cannabis in the past in Dublin, but it either made me ill or I would simply fall asleep. Whatever was in the stuff at Westville, it had a foul odour of turf, which left my eyes red raw. It would leave me with a headache that lasted until I could get some fresh air the following day. The obnoxious mix also acted as a prelude for evening activities amongst the natives.

In a sinister action, members began bringing in the newspapers to the prisoners specifically aimed at me with the usual headlines, 'Gay Alien Gets Jail' and 'Irish Gay Activist Gets Jail' and editorials on all matters pertaining to the corruption at the Department of Home Affairs. I began to become the subject of ridicule and defamatory remarks, which depressed me. In another twist, I was introduced to Azeez, who was originally from Lagos, Nigeria, who told me he was a staunch Muslim whose religion denounced homosexuality, drinking and smoking. I informed him that I was very much aware of Islam and their rules and regulations, but I asked him where in his litany of righteousness did it denounce theft, fraud and corruption as committed by Habib Khan and the Mansoors. In a state of silent reflection, Azeez retorted, "Of course, I personally have no objection to the lifestyle of gays." The friendship between the two of us was frosty for the remainder of my stay.

I told Bull of my experiences and he decided that I should not go into the yard alone and that I should be accompanied to the kitchens each day, where we lined up in twos and descended through the prison down the winding open stairwell to an open hall. However I rarely ate anything and relied on food from my family which was strictly limited.

'Dead Men Walking' is how they described the poor unfortunate sufferers of HIV/AIDS. It was now so common that the victims became statistics. One day I decided whilst there was no one was looking and my protectors were smoking dagga, I would go and speak to the frail men of circumstance. They were astonished that I should mingle with them and I was apprehensive as to whether they would speak to me, so I offered all of them a cigarette each, which helped to break the ice and a friendly conversation pursued.

These young men ranging from seventeen years to twenty years of age, were simply like the character ET, with no real flesh on their bones, drooping vacant watery eyes and no energy. They received little medication and what they did receive was inadequate. They were all former drug addicts and it was their addiction which had led them into a life of crime and was responsible for their incarceration as a result of carjacking, kidnapping and extortion. At this very young age, they had committed these horrendous crimes but in their own words "God has punished us." I told them that they must pray to God and to the Mother of God and then I stopped and thought, "What am I saying?" However, ironically one looked at me with sorrow in his tearful eyes, stretched out his hand and said, "It is alright, we are Christians," at which point they recited the Lord's Prayer. As they recited it in low, solemn voices, my guardian angels had arrived and it was time for me to return to my cell. Sadly, three of these young men passed away during my tenure at Westville.

Due to the constant violent attacks on prisoners at Westville, I had four prisoners as bodyguards assigned by Bull, two at the front and two behind, whom I repaid with cigarettes. On one occasion, on the way back from the well-lit, but gloomy kitchen, we weren't paying much attention when two blacks jumped on top of me, banging my head against the wall. There was a scuffle between prisoners, with whistles blowing from the members and the whole line-up running into disarray. The grim-looking members restrained the attackers and made an example by beating them severely on the buttocks, legs, arms and shoulders, whilst a strongly-built member slapped their faces repeatedly. They lost all their privileges, which meant no visits and isolation for seven days.

The separation from my family and friends and the seclusion from the outside world was devastatingly depressing. I was isolated in a foreign land, imprisoned by a corrupt regime, with a broken heart and spirit. I thought at one stage that I would not survive in my African prison hellhole. In all of the threats of death, I wished at one point with regret that they had not been carried out; a selfish but true thought. I thought to myself that I would be free from the hellhole and the degrading inhumane conditions to which I was being subjected. At the time, I actually envied the prisoners who committed suicide; they were brave, not cowards as some people would consider. They were free of their agony, but I was not brave enough. I was a coward. Why should I surrender my life for these warped and corrupt individuals who had taken everything from me with the exception of my soul? I decided to leave them in the hands of God and prayed for strength.

It was time for Bull to leave the prison after his ten-year tenure, he felt institutionalised and although he was somewhat scared of facing the world again, he was looking forward to his freedom.

At 7am on a cold wet morning three weeks following his departure, the members rushed into the cell and told all the prisoners except me to strip naked. I stood there watching as all the prisoners were told to bend over and tip their toes as a vicious sadistic-looking member with plastic gloves searched them for drugs. A humiliating and undignified procedure, but essential in their quest for seeking out the harder drugs smuggled into the prison. There was a full-scale search of the cell and the prisoners, before we were informed that Bull had been shot dead in a feud the night before in Chatsworth. The prisoners who had known him for so long were uncontrollably shocked and devastated. I was grateful to Bull for his kindness and protection of me. May he rest in peace. I was extremely perturbed at this continuing scale of violence and death. I prayed like I've never prayed before for God to release me.

In the meantime at the Court of Appeal, a Judge Winchester, expressed grave concern over my case and ordered that it be heard as soon as possible. The date was set for the 9 July 2002, at 9am at Pietermaritzburg, 79 kilometres from Durban. There was an agonising 39 days left and it was the longest period in my life. Advocate Howse busily prepared the Heads of Argument for my release.

In the midst of despair we were joined in the cell by the commander inmate of the wing, known as Baby Face. He was 28 years old with bushy black hair, missing teeth and a body covered in tattoos. He was a vicious little thug of 5' 4" in stature who had spent most of his life behind bars in various prisons throughout South Africa. He had numerous convictions under his belt including rape, murder, theft and arson. He had started life as a petty thief after his parents abandoned him in Cape Town and worked at an early age as a floor tiler. By day, he was tiling the floors of his clients and by night he was robbing their homes and premises. In the daylight hours, he had the advantage of sizing up the house or property for his eagle-like descent during the night. He had the most piercing voice that bellowed through the day and night like a rat clenched between a cat's teeth. It was from early morning until late at night that he smoked dagga, preying on young black victims to do his dirty work (such as stealing the dagga), or else facing the wrath of his physical brutal torture. He had demanded elevation from cell B403 to B401 because the latter had a television set, or so we were led to believe. He demanded to see programmes of his choice and often denied the Zulus in the cell the privilege of watching Xhosa News or programmes of their culture. In the evening, he would mix dagga, tobacco and mandrax, and smoke from a filthy pipe wrapped in an equally filthy cloth. He would scream in ecstasy as his eyes bulged hideously from his head. Although head of the inmates in the cell, Ravi was often overshadowed by the dwarfed thug, a parasite who cared only for himself.

On the one and only occasion that I fell into a deep sleep, I was suddenly awoken in the middle of the night with the hands of Baby Face wrapped firmly around my mouth and testicles. He warned me not to have any backlash against the Mansoors. This action confirmed that they were far more powerful than anticipated. He further went on to tell me that my advocate Jimmy

Howse would be assassinated and I would be demoted to live with the blacks in a cell at the bottom of the wing where Charlie was raped; he said, "and you know what happens there."

My spirit was challenged, which left me with low self-esteem. It seemed I was completely vulnerable, as this warp-minded criminal was not going to give up. I decided to say nothing and considered my next move.

Baboo was his best friend and I thought I should mention it to him, but on the day I was going to tell him, I was thrown against the wall, as two black inmates grabbed hold of Baboo. In a military-style punishment, Baby Face had ordered his two soldiers from the famous gang of 28 to execute his orders on Baboo for stealing dagga. In front of the whole cell, whilst the gates were unlocked, Baboo was stripped naked, his arms and legs were spread apart and he was lashed on his back and buttocks several times. He was then ordered to stand to attention as part of their so-called army punishment, whilst the soldier clasped his right hand thump back and with precision struck Baboo downwards on both sides of his face. He was marked on the back and buttocks and blood trickled down his face. It was over in less than three minutes, leaving a humiliated man in pain and shock, with a firm lesson that one soldier does not steal from another.

I thought the best way of humouring Baby Face would be to give him his own supply of cigarettes, because they were like gold dust. If I supplied him with a carton of cigarettes every week, he would give the two fingers to the member who was trying to buy him on behalf of the Mansoors. It worked.

Baby Face had attained his position on the wing by virtue of intimidation and the longevity of his sentence in various prisons and he had attained the strange title of Commander In Chief. He was a malicious man with a warped mind who disliked Nelson Mandela intensely for not doing enough for the blacks when he gained power.

On another occasion we were surprised when the evening news featured a segment of a prison at Bloemfontein, 398 kilometres from Johannesburg or 634 kilometres from Durban. It showed actual film footage, which was beamed around the world, of the members selling dagga, alcohol, cigarettes, boys for sex and a gun for 700 rands (£70 in those days), to wealthy prisoners. It showed explicit scenes of one teenager stripping naked for another prisoner and getting in position for a sexual act. The biggest controversy of all was the actual gun. It was a devastating blow to the prison system in South Africa.

The Prison Governor was so incensed by corruption within government circles and in the prison system itself that he allowed the prisoners to take the film footage. The prisoners at Westville were delighted with the report. The members who featured in the report became guests of the government in many of their prison institutions. The Governor was transferred and then dismissed. The South African Parliament debated the issue and hoped it would fade into oblivion, but prisoners have long memories and members were subjected to violent attacks from the gangs within the prison, causing riots and mayhem. It was a classic piece of television and the best exposure to date.

On the eve of my appeal, I tossed and turned and prayed for a successful result at the South African High

Court of Appeal. It was a tense night and my mind was racing in all directions. What would the outcome be? What if everything went wrong? I noticed extra members with guard dogs and I became paranoid.

I was not strong enough to live in a prison, particularly in the knowledge that I was innocent. I had been subjected to the lowest form of indignation, surrounded by so much violence, disease, death and depravity that my spirit was finally about to shatter.

I wished I had never gone to South Africa and I could neither think of forgiveness or hatred of the perpetrators because I simply did not know my own mind on that wretched night of hell. As dawn broke, I somehow felt a slight sense of spiritual comfort and began to think positively once again. Someone once said, "Only when man is in the deepest valley, does he realise how glorious it is to be on the highest mountain."

TWENTY-ONE

"We accept that he did not initiate the fake marriage."
High Court of Appeal. 9 July 2002

As I waited patiently in my overcrowded cell at Westville on the calm but overcast morning of 9 July 2002, my family and friends set out on the 79 kilometres drive to Pietermaritzburg and the High Court of Appeal. They were met by my advocate Jimmy Howse and my lawyer Pregasen Marimuthu, equipped with 56, points, or heads of argument for my release. They were hoping with all their might that justice would ring out loud in a land so often deaf and blind to truths and the miscarriages of justice. It was exactly 77 days to the very day of my arrest by the two corrupt Home Affairs' officials. However, it was on this day that they had no power over two judges, Ronald McLaren and Christopher Nicholson.

The family and team led by the eminent advocate took their places inside the courtroom as the esteemed judges took their seats on the bench. My sister, Yvonne, said her heart was racing and the atmosphere was tense, until Advocate Howse arose and delivered an impeccable summarisation of events, and then outlined in precise detail his heads of argument for my release. The young Pregasen Marimuthu, faithfully seated next to him, made notes on crucial points. The judges listened attentively, whilst occasionally making notes. My sister watched the expression of their faces; she watched their every move, every blink of the eye, nervously awaiting their reaction. The long conscious delivery by the eminent advocate commenced: "It is submitted that the sentence on Counts 2 and 3 is vitiated by error and/or misdirection. It is further submitted that the sentence is so severe that it induces a sense of shock. Alternatively it is so different from the sentence, which the above Honourable Court would have imposed, that it merits intervention on appeal.

"It is submitted that the learned Regional Magistrate misdirected herself, in that she overlooked certain facts of cardinal importance. The first of these is the fact that the Appellant did not initiate the wrongdoings surrounding his application for immigration and only acquiesced those wrongdoings when it comes to his attention that Habib Khan had (of his own volition and without the authority of the Appellant) obtained the falsified marriage certificate. It is to be noted that, in her judgement of sentence, the learned Regional Magistrate did not once mention nor allude to the fact that the Appellant did not initiate the crimes in Counts 2 and 3 [fraud and corruption].

"The Appellant had engaged the assistance of a reputable firm, namely Acutts, to assist him in lawfully expediting his immigration. Acutts referred the Appellant to Peter Joubert and Habib Khan. The Appellant then enlisted their assistance in order to arrange his immigration lawfully. The Appellant was accordingly not accountable for Habib Khan's actions in procuring the false marriage certificate. The misdirection by the learned Regional Magistrate is further illustrated by the following passage from her judgment:

'The court has no cogent reason for why the accused did not make proper application through the correct channels for his residence permit.'

"To the contrary, the evidence proves firstly that the Appellant acted in good faith in engaging agents to make a lawful application for immigration on his behalf."

Advocate Howes continued with lengthy legal arguments quoting similar circumstances and referring back to the Regional Magistrate.

"It is submitted that the learned Regional Magistrate ought to have found that because the Appellant did not initiate the wrongdoings and because he was strongly tempted to acquiesce in the conduct of the principal offenders, his crimes were considerably mitigated. It is respectfully submitted that if the learned Regional Magistrate had taken those factors into account she would have inevitably come to a different conclusion regarding the most appropriate sentence.

"Regarding the corruption charge (Count 3), which the learned Regional Magistrate described as the most 'heinous' of all three offences, she completely overlooked the fact that the Appellant did not personally bribe the Home Affairs' official concerned. The learned Regional Magistrate's judgement is devoid of any reference to this material fact. The Appellant furthermore made it clear in his evidence that he had received the reassurance of the Mansoors that they would look after the entire matter.

"The Appellant can, therefore, not be described as a chief perpetrator of the corruption. To the contrary, he did not instruct Ismail Mansoor to commit a crime, nor did he know what Mansoor was going to do at the Department of Home Affairs. Mansoor was left to his own devices and perpetrated the corruption of his own volition. The Appellant's participation was peripheral and amounts to no more than acquiescing in what Ismail Mansoor did, subject to the assurances by the Mansoors that they would look after the whole matter.

"It is submitted that in these circumstances, the Appellant did not act in the knowledge that he was committing a crime so heinous that upon his arrest he would be in line for a term of direct imprisonment. It is submitted that if the learned Regional Magistrate had acquired a proper insight to the Appellant's participation in the offence, she would have sentenced him altogether differently.

"Further absent from the learned Regional Magistrate's judgment is any comment on the State's conspicuous failure to prosecute Ismail Mansoor, who was the initiator and chief perpetrator of the corruption and has always been available to the State to be indicted and punished for his role in the crime.

"It is conceded that the fraudulent 'marriage' between the Appellant and Muniaama Moodley is an aggravating feature. It is, however, submitted that the learned Regional Magistrate misdirected herself regarding the extent of the aggravation created by this feature. The learned Regional Magistrate stated, *'The court is aware that a person of strong religious faith, such as Mrs Moodley, will find immense embarrassment and humiliation if her close community discovers that she is married, especially to a white foreigner.'*

"The awareness that the learned Religion Magistrate had of Mrs Moodley's embarrassment and humiliation was not based on any evidence that was presented during the trial. The learned Regional Magistrate appears to have found furthermore that the Appellant being a white foreigner is part of the reason for Mrs Moodley's embarrassment and humiliation. It is respectfully submitted that these findings are inconsistent with universally acceptable religions or racial values, and accordingly ought not to have been held against the Appellant as aggravating factors.

"It is further submitted that the learned Regional Magistrate exaggerated Mrs Moodley's trauma. The evidence reveals that Mrs Moodley had considerable difficulty motivating why the crimes in question had a significant effect on her."

The whole truth of my predicament was thrashed out in the Court of Appeal and I found it strange that these arguments were lost in the regional court. I was acutely aware that the Regional Magistrate didn't like me and she always appeared awkward and nervous. Mr Howes continued, "It is submitted that the Regional Magistrate misdirected herself by assuming an incorrect perception of the Appellant's character and that her approach to sentencing was negatively influenced by this perception."

He then went on to reprehend her over the interdict of Ahmed Yacoob Mansoor when he said, "The learned Regional Magistrate had no business relying on exhibit H as evidence of the Appellant's questionable character. The interim order was obtained as a result of an ex-parte application. The Appellant made it clear that he had not seen the allegations upon which the application was founded, nor had he been afforded the opportunity to respond to them. What is more, the Appellant denied the allegations. It is submitted that the aforementioned misdirections by the learned Regional Magistrate had the result that she sentenced the Appellant more severely than she would have done on a proper appraisal of the evidence before her."

In relation to her inappropriate language involving me and the interests of society, Advocate Howse quoted her remarks to the Appeal Court judges, who apparently were looking more bemused as the delivery continued, *"The number of illegal aliens in our country creates various socio-economic problems. The interests of society must also be considered and the South African community has come to view these foreigners in a hostile light as they usurp employment in basic communities. Furthermore they have been involved in criminal activity on behalf of international cartels or syndicates."*

Mr Howse continued, "The above comments may be correct as regards the general problem that the Republic of South Africa has with illegal aliens. The learned Regional Magistrate's comments are, however, entirely irrelevant to the Appellant's case, which is unique in that he does not fall into the category of aliens described by the learned Regional Magistrate. That he does not fall into that category was clearly established by the evidence and argument of counsel."

In a clear, precise voice, he informed the Court, "It is respectively submitted that the Appellant has already suffered more than enough in this case and that his suffering is the result of a misapprehension of the facts of the case and an inability to distinguish them from the problem cases that plague our society. Of his experience in this case the Appellant stated, *'I have never known anything like this. The only time I have seen something similar was on the television or in the movies.'*

"It must be noted that Muniaama Moodley was prepared to accept his apology. It is submitted that the finding by the learned Regional Magistrate that Mrs

Moodley's forgiveness of the Appellant was the result of repeated questioning by the defence is patently wrong."

Mr Howse then went on to read cases of law dating back to 1960 to 2001 and said, "It is accordingly submitted that the learned Regional Magistrate misdirected herself regarding the seriousness of the offences and the authority provided by the decisions upon which she relied. It is respectively submitted that the learned Regional Magistrate's reasoning is unsound and constitutes misdirection and is unsound for further reason that even a wealthy businessman can be significantly punished by a properly calculated fine. It is accordingly submitted that the learned Regional Magistrate misdirected herself regarding the suitability of a fine."

As the packed courtroom listened in silence to the eloquent delivery by the distinguished advocate, he said, "It is important to remember that the Appellant does not fall into that category of aliens who represent an ongoing problem to the authorities in the country. The Appellant's situation is unique in that he was eligible to immigrate lawfully and would have been accepted into the country if his prescribed lawful instructions had been adhered to. It is submitted that this is not the problem crime plaguing the country at present and is therefore not the conduct to be addressed by means of an exemplary sentence.

"The question that the Regional Magistrate ought to have asked herself is whether it was appropriate to use the Appellant as an example to those who, in circumstances which are entirely different from the Appellant's, enter the country illegally. The result of the learned Regional Magistrate's misdirection is that she used the Appellant as a means to deter others from doing something that the Appellant himself did not do. The Chief Immigration Officer went on to say that he is unaware of any similar case where an offender has been imprisoned. It would appear, therefore, that the learned Regional Magistrate sought to use the Appellant's case as the first of its kind.

"It is submitted that the Appellant ought not to have been sacrificed on the altar of deterrence. As important as the factors of prevalence and general deterrence are, they must not be permitted to weigh so heavily as to negate other factors, which lessen the gravity of the offence in the particular circumstances of the case before the court."

As he was bringing his arguments to a close, he stated categorically, "The Appellant is a respectable person of some standing in the community and is not the sort of person to be imprisoned unless to do so is absolutely necessary. It is respectively submitted that the errors and misdirections by the learned Regional Magistrate are such that they have resulted in her imposing an entirely inappropriate sentence in respect of Counts 2 and 3. Finally, it is further submitted that the sentence is such that it would induce a sense of shock in any right thinking member of society. It is submitted that the sentence is so different from the one the above Honourable Court would have considered appropriate, that it merits intervention."

The two High Court Appeal judges, McLaren and Nicholson, who had read through the trial transcripts and the heads of arguments prior to the sitting of 9 July 2002, appeared both impressed and displeased at what they had heard from the advocate. They were impressed by the advocate's superb and professional presentation, but discontented with the way the Regional Magistrate had conducted the hearing and the ultimate sentence itself. This was evident in their final written judgment of events.

There was a silent pause before they spoke and said, "We accept that he did not initiate the fake marriage or the documents. We also accept that the Regional Magistrate misdirected herself in that she overlooked certain facts of cardinal importance. The description of the crime by the Regional Magistrate as 'heinous' was inappropriate and exaggerated. He has been the victim of the machinations of the Mansoor family and she ought to have taken that into account. Therefore, we order his immediate release and a warrant of liberation served on the prison forthwith. We will break for lunch and deliver our judgment in full after the break."

It was exactly 12.41pm when the judges' voices were drowned by cheers, applause and tears of joy. The two judges looked amused by the reaction their verdict had on a well-behaved court room, who were now celebrating victory. My sister Yvonne shouted her gratification with tears strolling down her cheeks as they nodded in gesture and departed the bench.

At 12.55pm, unaware of the Court's decision and the jubilation, I telephoned Yvonne on her cell phone. Shaun answered without telling me anything, but I could hear a scuffle for the phone as my heart was beating nervously. Yvonne, bless heart, burst into tears, crying joyfully, "We won, we won, you're free darling and there is no deportation, you are not being deported… hold on."

Advocate Jimmy Howse took over the phone and in a gentle, but firm voice said, "Liam, I can only say how sorry I am for this whole dreadful ordeal. My colleagues and I are relieved to see an end to this crisis. I can only apologise to you from all right-thinking South Africans and I hope you can pick up your life where you left off. We will get you out of that prison now."

In an overjoyed state, I thanked him and Pregasen for all the work they had done on my behalf and then I immediately telephoned my mother in Dublin to break the news. She cried with relief.

TWENTY-TWO

"The effect of the Magistrate's sentence was that of an indignant censor using a sledgehammer." Court of Appeal, 9 July 2002

As the judges resumed to deliver their judgment a fax had been sent to Westville prison for my release but we had to wait some hours for the original. In the meantime they continued:

"It is only trite law that this Court can only interfere with a sentence imposed by a lower court if there is misdirection by the Magistrate, or the sentence is disturbingly inappropriate. Mr Howse submitted that the Magistrate misdirected herself in several material respects, warranting interference by this Court.

"The first, related to the fact that the Appellant did not initiate the fraud and bribery, is a prominent gay businessman who entered the country on 9 October, 2001, to settle and set up a business. He was clearly a man of considerable means and brought in more than a million rands for that purpose. The Appellant's bank statement, which was handed in at the hearing as an exhibit, also makes it clear that the appellant paid 600,000 rands [£60,000 in those days] to a person referred to as A Y Mansoor on 24 December 2001. The Appellant met the Mansoor family some years ago, who offered to obtain a temporary residence permit from the Department of Home Affairs for him. The payment of the 600,000 rands to the Mansoor family was a deposit on a property the Appellant intended purchasing. In order to speed up the occupation, the Appellant was persuaded to part with 80,000 rands [£8,000 in those days] for a grand piano belonging to the owner of the property he was purchasing, but he later discovered that Yacoob Mansoor had pocketed half of that sum and not handed it over to the owner. I understand from the evidence led, that the deal for the purchase of the house went sour and the Mansoors have refused to refund the 600,000 rands to the Appellant.

"On the 7 April, the Appellant received a letter from the Mansoors in which repayment of the deposit is refuted and additional sums of 650,000 rands [£65,000 in those days] for what was termed 'transfer costs, disbursements' and something referred to as 'Sadek's disposal in terms of the second mandate' are claimed. In addition, in the letter an application is threatened in the High Court if the money is not paid. The letter continued to record that notice would be given to the Department of Home Affairs to establish if the Appellant was an alien, the identity of the woman to whom he was married and the South African police or Interpol to establish whether he was wanted for any criminal investigation.

"It was a clear attempt to blackmail the Appellant and he testified that he was certain that, in addition to this, it was the Mansoors who reported him to the Department. The magistrate also took into account the fact that the South African community has come to view illegal aliens with hostility, because they involve themselves in criminal activities and take away jobs. This was also a misdirection as the Appellant does not fit into this sort of stereotype. In fact, had he been able to set up his business, he would have been able to employ South African citizens.

"Mrs Moodley testified as to what her feelings were when she discovered that she was married to the Appellant. The court found that a person of such religious belief would feel, 'immense embarrassment and humiliation if her close community discovers that she is now married, especially to a white foreigner'. What is apparent is that the officials of the Department came to Mrs Moodley and told her that she was married to the Appellant, as a result of the deception by Khan. Instead of explaining that she was the victim and that the fraudulent marriage could have no consequence, I get the impression they emphasised to her how hurt she must feel. While it is unfortunate that her name was used, no other adverse consequences accrued to her and she was not prejudiced, apart from the shock of hearing the facts of the matter. The magistrate overemphasised her pain and suffering and misdirected herself in this regard as well."

"It seems to me," said Judge J. McLaren, "that the law should also be directing its judicial wrath at the government officials who perpetrate the corrupt practice, as their role encompasses greater moral turpitude. I rather doubt that the sentence would have come to the notice of the hordes of illegal immigrants in this country, let alone deterred them effectively.

"The effect of the Magistrate's sentence was that of an indignant censor using a sledgehammer, to paraphrase the erstwhile Chief Justice of this country. Sentencing requires a balanced approach that eschews the overemphasis of any of the three cardinal foci of sentence, namely the offender, the offence and the interests of society. The Appellant, was a victim of the machinations of the Mansoor family and the magistrate ought to have taken that into account. For these reasons, it seems to me that the magistrate seriously misdirected herself in the respects mentioned."

Meanwhile, back at Westville, I waited for my family to arrive which was taking longer than expected and I feared that something was wrong. It transpired that the Durban Regional Court was either refusing or delaying to sign the papers for the prison but in any event my legal team had to ask the Appeal Court to intervene and request that they comply with the order of the court.

At 4.50pm on the afternoon of 9 July 2002, I walked through the gates, out into the reception area of Westville prison, through the open door and into the arms of my beloved family. It was the happiest moment of my life. The nightmare was over or was it?

I had had enough of South Africa and I decided to return home to Ireland, not before giving one interview to South Africa's *Sunday Times*, providing it was published after my departure. The detrimental psychological effect that the experience had on me and my family was overwhelming and it took its toll on my mother's life forever.

On Friday 13 July 2002, I left our family home in Mobeni Heights for Durban International Airport for a flight to Johannesburg and onwards to London Heathrow and Dublin. I was accompanied by my family and my other brother-in-law's brother Eric, who was a Captain at the time in the South African Police. The situation had been so volatile that we feared another trumped-up charge by the Mansoors or an attack, and so

Eric decided to travel to Johannesburg with me until the plane was safely airborne en route to Europe.

Eric, a professional policeman to his fingertips, was more concerned for my safety. It wouldn't have been a surprise to any of us if a deranged gunman had come charging out of nowhere. There was tension in the air as the last call for boarding was announced and I had to endure the painful goodbye to Yvonne and Naren, and my nephew and nieces, before forwarding to the departure gate. I was distraught and tormented by fears that the Mansoors might strike at the last minute, at the final port of departure, Johannesburg.

After landing we had two hours together, and when it was time to check in with Virgin Atlantic flight VS602 to London we said our goodbyes and I thanked him for his support and help as he stood behind the security belt. I approached the black security official with my emergency passport. He looked at me suspiciously and confidently informed me that under no circumstances could I travel on the document. The dreaded moment had arrived, or so I thought, as he looked me up and down. I told him that it was a legitimate document from the Irish Embassy in Pretoria, but he continued to argue. I told him that I had the cell number of an official from the Irish Embassy, Laurence Simms, which he could ring to clear the matter.

He walked away for a moment as I wondered what I would do if I was delayed any further. Eric followed him and asked to see his superior and within the blink of an eye the red carpet was rolled out and I was on board waiting for take-off.

The doors closed, the plane taxied out and she raced up the runway like a magnificent bird flying out over the city of Johannesburg and the Drakensberg. I looked down on the land where I had planned to build a new future and participate in a new developing nation. I thought of that land now enduring its own hell at the hands of corrupt politicians and their associates. The Cry for Freedom had been drowned by the triumphant cheers of lustful men, attaining power and ignoring those who helped them to achieve their ambitions. From the tall glass buildings in the wealth of the cities and suburbs to the shacks in the shantytowns of disease-riddled squalor, suffocated by poverty and starvation. South Africa is a beautiful multifaceted land where the ideals and realisms of Nelson Mandela have been suffocated in a web of deceit, greed, conspiracies, corruption, violence and death. The natural overwhelming beauty of this land with its gregarious people is lost in the shadow of the gun. Will I ever forgive these men of evil or could I ever forgive them? One thing is certain, I will never forget.

EPILOGUE

I have heard it said that I was the author of my own misfortune which is highly debateable! Firstly I was extremely vulnerable following my separation after a quarter of a century with Tony. The perpetrators saw through this vulnerability like the eye of a tiger. Secondly I invested a quantum of trust in so-called family friends. In hindsight the charge against me was false, tainted and sullied. On the flip side I was naïve and stupid to have trusted too many too late!

The realisation and effect of the whole ordeal hit me like a ton of bricks when I returned to Ireland. Our family doctor, Fergus Purcell came immediately to examine me and was responsible for restoring me to good health for which I have been forever grateful. Initially, I experienced dreadful bouts of depression and nightmares but I refused anti-depression tablets and fought the anxiety myself. I am forever grateful to the many good people of South Africa including family and friends who sent me messages of good will.

It was gratifying to have my liberty and freedom and the love of my family and extended family who united around me in support of my recuperation. My mother was thrilled beyond belief to have me home but the experience had a lasting effect on her and she became ill. I always looked after her and was constantly by her side but another tragedy was to hit us on the 12 February 2006, my South African brother-in-law, Derek died suddenly leaving my sister with three young children to raise. One year and three days later, 15 February 2007, my beloved former partner of twenty-five years, Tony Keogan died suddenly. We were plunged into a deep and darkened place and my mother's health worsened. She was in and out of hospital and became a shadow of her former self.

Throughout her life she had been such a lively vibrant woman who had travelled the world and was very supportive of me as a gay man along with my peers. She was exactly like her mother before her, my beloved grandmother Lambe, a hard-working liberated woman who would help anyone at any time. In the late 1970s, a young man, a customer of our club, approached my mother for advice. He told her of his turbulent relationship with his father regarding his sexuality which was quite the norm in Irish society when a father found that one of his children was gay. He asked her if she would meet him and although reluctant at first she discussed it with Tony and me and agreed to meet this man.

Three days later I travelled with my mother and Tony to a north county Dublin council estate where we were greeted by the young man. My mother entered the house whilst Tony and I remained outside in the car. Twenty minutes passed when his mother came out and invited us in; although apprehensive, we went into the house. My mother was engaged in deep conversation with the young man and his father in the privacy of the parlour. I was beginning to wonder if this was a good idea when the door swung open and the young man with my mother and his father entered the sitting room. He turned to his wife and said, "Well Marie, I'm prepared to give this a go! We're off to the gay club on Saturday night." The young man was delighted and his mother was thrilled.

On the way back, I asked my mother, "Could you not have picked a quieter night other than Saturday?" To which came the reply, "The busiest the better, so that they realise that gay people are part of society." They came as arranged and had a wonderful time with my mother arranging for all of us to meet up in Bartley Dunne's a week later. The young man eventually met someone and moved to Sydney, Australia, where Tony and I met them both in 1989. We asked Mum how she had managed to convert his father and she replied, "A mother's instinct, the auld geezer felt his masculinity was threatened, I soon put him straight on that one!" No more was said about the matter.

Upon reflection of my own novitiate years of 'coming out' as a gay man, it was extremely difficult back in Ireland of the 1960s or even mainland Europe for that matter to actually say, "I am homosexual" which was in effect against the law and punishable by life imprisonment. In some Islamic countries today, it is death by hanging, which is both horrifying and deplorable. The Roman Catholic Church in collaboration with the Irish state ran the country hand-in-hand and the dominance of the church had a great critical effect on people's lives. We have heard about sexual abuse after sexual abuse, the mother and baby homes and the Magdalene laundries along with the children of priests.

It was against this dominant force that brave men and women set out to change the law on the Victorian 1861, Offences against the Person Act, whilst Tony and I opened the first gay commercial night club to the astonishment of many in 1975. We began to claim our identity in society whilst encouraging others to do the same. Courage in the darkness of despair is the backbone of strength, and courage lies within all of us. In the passage of time, due to the persistent work of David Norris, homosexuality was legalised in Ireland in 1993.

On 23 September 1993, Tony and I opened the first gay bed and breakfast, with Danny La Rue cutting the ribbon. The gay community became stronger and the nation voted in a referendum in favour for equal marriage in 2015. It was a unique move that helped change people's attitudes and along with other ventures we had created, it permeated the way for Irish gay commercial life.

On 10 May 2012, my mother's lifelong friend and neighbour and a very good friend to me, Maureen, died. Maureen had been with us during the crisis in South Africa and had challenged the Mansoors on several occasions. Life was passing us by and my mother missed her immensely.

In July 2013, she was hospitalised again and I would spend hours with her in her private ward. One particular sweltering sunny afternoon I left early and within an hour I received a telephone call to return to the hospital as my beloved mother had little time left. I was stunned beyond belief as she appeared to be fine when I left her. My sister, Denise and two of her children rushed with me to the hospital followed by our dear friends Breda and Desmond. We were taken into a 'family' room where this young doctor emphasised that my mother's organs were closing down. I didn't believe him.

My niece had sent a message to our family in South Africa during the shock meeting. Within minutes my sister, Yvonne telephoned me on my mobile and said her husband, my brother-in-law, Naren wished to speak with the doctor. He enquired what medication she was on and suggested that her treatment be changed. The doctor refused. When they got back to me they said they would be in Dublin in less than forty-eight hours. Time was of the essence and so all the extended family were informed with her sister, my aunt Evelyn travelling from Seattle.

When Yvonne and Naren arrived in from South Africa, Naren spoke with the chief consultant who agreed to change her medication. The consultant informed me that I needed to get her to a nursing home but this suggestion was off the table. My mother had always asked me never to shift her to a home and I never did. I informed the consultant that the idea was scrapped and although I insisted that the intention was good, I would personally look after my mother doing all things that carers do and I did it 24/7. My mother left the hospital for the comfort of her own home. I brought in all the aid she required including a stair lift which she loved. She lived for nearly another three years.

In 2015, she had prayed for a 'YES' vote in the marriage equality referendum and as I sat beside her holding her hand the tears of joy strolled down her cheeks when the result was announced in favour of the 'YES' vote. She said she was very grateful to Almighty God that she lived to see the day.

By Christmas 2015, she was diagnosed with cancer and commenced radiation in January 2016. She was given twelve months to live and as time went on she became very frail. I could never leave her alone as she became agitated and all she wanted to do was hold my hand. She would reminisce about the horrors of South Africa and prayed to God to forgive the perpetrators. Then she turned to me and said, "Son, you must find it in your heart to forgive because God wouldn't like you carrying that grudge." The assistance we received from the Palliative care team at Our Lady's Hospice, Harold's Cross was immeasurable.

The extended family were becoming worried that my caring job was becoming all too time-consuming and one family member, since deceased said, "But you are sacrificing your life!" The sacrifice as suggested was no sacrifice at all. My mother was the pearl of my life and never caused me an ounce of bother. I devoted my time and effort in trying to appease her pain and make life as comfortable as possible. She became so tired in early evening that I would have to take her to bed at 5pm. She wouldn't sleep unless she knew I was next to her. With the intense medication she was on, she would drift in and out of consciousness and when I would lift her in and out of bed throughout the night, she would smile and say, "It's like having a dance son, those were the days."

At the beginning of May 2016, she knew she was dying but reassured me that we would be together again in the not too distant future. 09 May 2016 at 12.20pm she smiled and closed her eyes. I felt an overwhelming spiritual feeling, one that I had never experienced before. An hour before she left us she whispered something in my ear which will go to my grave with me. It was not only the saddest day of my life but it was also the most memorable, spiritual segment of my life which gave me strength and courage to accept her passing and continue with my life. That strength and blessing I received that day has never faltered. It was a mesmerising miraculous experience which transfixed my life forever.

One hears of people claiming to have seen apparitions and they are ridiculed. I saw no apparitions but the teachings of my mother and grandmother that "God is within the temple of your soul," manifested itself that day.

It is only prudent that I acknowledge the vast amount of people I have met throughout my lifetime, far too many to mention in this memoir, but please be assured that you are in my thoughts and I thank you all for travelling that journey with me. My journey throughout the decades has been filled with ups and downs, agonies and ecstasies but the underlining element of my strength is my faith in God. The natural beauty and wisdom of my mother's love, whose soul shone through her eyes, was immense. For my beloved Tony Keogan with whom I shared a quarter of a century, he was the treasure of my life, a magnitude of support and the love and only love of my lifetime. I miss him dearly. To my family and extended family, where would I be without you? Thank you for your love and support. I would like to thank my lifelong friend Alex Carroll, of forty-seven years, for his friendship, loyalty and encouragement.

Human beings have human nature often animalistic at times when oppressed, as I saw at Westville prison. However I would like to think that the majority of human beings are honest, decent souls who would cause no offence to anyone. In my days as an entrepreneur, I soon learned that there is no sentiment in business but there is an enormous difference between sentiment and fraud which the perpetrators subjected me to. The stress, agony and torture that I endured with their blessing and who were later castigated by the Court of Appeal will never be forgotten. However as a Spiritual Christian, I forgive those who conspired to offend and harm me and I leave their fate in the hands of Almighty God.

The treks and trails of life are measured not how we start but how we finish and for the first time in my life, I am experiencing inner peace which allows me to forgive. Martin Luther King Jr, once said, "We must develop and maintain the capacity to forgive. He who is devoid of the power to forgive is devoid of the power to love. There is good in the worst of us and some evil in the best of us. When we discover this, we are less prone to hate our enemies."

Author – Liam Ledwidge at his home in Dublin, Ireland.

Lightning Source UK Ltd.
Milton Keynes UK
UKHW020654140122
397094UK00006B/206